Potten Baber + Murray
14 pix as 8pp on
2 x 4pp wraps

Sigourney Weaver

Sigourney Weaver

ROBERT SELLERS

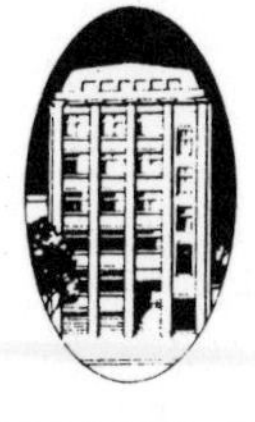

ROBERT HALE · LONDON

First published in Great Britain 1992

ISBN 0 7090 4454 2

Robert Hale Limited
Clerkenwell House
Clerkenwell Green
London EC1R 0HT

Set in Sabon by
Derek Doyle & Associates, Mold, Clwyd.
Printed in Great Britain by
St Edmundsbury Press, Bury St Edmunds, Suffolk.
Bound by Hunter and Foulis.

Contents

List of Illustrations

PICTURE CREDITS

The Kobal Collection: 1, 3, 4; Rank Organisation PLC: 2; London Features International: 5, 7, 10, 12; Camera Press: 6, 8, 11; Rex Features: 9; Pictorial Press Limited: 13, 14.

Foreword

The tell-tale signs of disappointment showed clearly on the face of Sigourney Weaver. The taste of defeat, a rare flavour for her, settled uncomfortably in her mouth. An evening which had begun full of bright hopes and promises had ended in abject failure and public embarrassment. The Academy Awards ceremony, that prince among self-congratulatory events, as much a part of Hollywood culture as the films themselves, had once again come round. This particular year, 1989, saw Sigourney nominated in two separate acting categories, a rare achievement matched by only a handful of other performers. For the devoted fan the event is an evening of unqualified joy, a jamboree which allows cherished glimpses of favourite celebrities. For the legion of lawyers, accountants, and businessmen who rule over Hollywood it is the most important night of the year: with millions of dollars of added box-office revenue going to the winning movies, they hold the spectacle in an almost religious reverence. Many stars regard the event with the same respectful esteem, happy to perpetuate the super-fragile myth of Tinseltown, willing victims of excess.

Sigourney Weaver, however, was unimpressed by all the false gloss; her deep theatrical roots were naturally at odds with the dumb showbiz razzmatazz that events like the Oscars exude in nauseating abundance. Ten years at the top and Sigourney chose to see herself more as a New York stage actress than a product of Hollywood. Film is not a temple at which Sigourney Weaver worships.

As she made her way towards the Shrine Auditorium in Los Angeles, her poised presence, intelligent features and sensual remoteness seemed almost to bring an air of normality to the plastic proceedings. Despite her ability to see through the ceremony's exterior to its decadent, hard centre, the actress was extremely flattered that her work had been acknowledged by the Academy and was clearly revelling in her moment of glory. Regally draped in a long sleek white Yves Saint Laurent dress, positively the best outfit of the evening, Sigourney Weaver walked past crowds of adoring fans (to whom she blew soft kisses), and lines of jostling pressmen with jealous eyes. Before the grand gathering of Tinseltown's beautiful people Sigourney was secretly confident of her chances, and justifiably so. She was favourite to snatch the Best Supporting Actress award for her amusing shenanigans in *Working Girl*, a dry and cruel parody of the ultimate office bitch which had already earned her numerous accolades. Even the eventual winner, Geena Davis, had expected Sigourney's name to be called. But her best chance of success lay with her portrayal of the animal conservationist Dian Fossey in *Gorillas in the Mist*, a spellbinding *tour de force* that made for compelling viewing. There were many critics and admirers who believed that the Best Actress Oscar belonged on Sigourney Weaver's mantelpiece. But the competition that year was surprisingly strong. While everyone expected Dustin Hoffman to win Best Actor for *Rain Man*, the contest for top actress was not so clear cut: all five nominees were equally likely to collect the statuette. Co-favourite with Weaver was her old rival Meryl Streep whose powerfully restrained performance as Lindy Chamberlin, the Australian housewife accused of murdering her own child in Fred Schepisi's *A Cry in the Dark*, was further testimony of her brilliance at character study. Glenn Close was another hot possibility: her ice-cold and sinister portrayal of the unscrupulous *marquise* in *Dangerous Liaisons* had taken the American cinemagoing public by storm, as had Melanie Griffith's antics as the scheming secretary in *Working Girl*. Ultimately it was the dark horse, Jodie Foster, playing a gang-rape victim in *The Accused*, who was to win.

On more than one occasion, Sigourney has made it known to reporters that she would rather settle for a cluster of nominations than just the one Oscar. 'It means you're getting a good range of roles.' But to miss out on the award, the highest honour a film actor can receive, twice in one night must have hurt her greatly. Gallant to the last, she did not publicly display her disappointment and calmly left the auditorium radiating the cool aloofness that had made her a star. Actually, her predicament was of acute humiliation. The actress had managed to entice her rather fragile parents away from their serene home in Santa Monica to attend the Oscar ceremony and, by the end of the evening, was a little embarrassed that they had come all that way for nothing.

Interestingly, the five nominees for Best Actress, bar the winner, were close contemporaries of Sigourney Weaver's. All of them had won the Academy's approval by portraying tough, liberated, and strong-willed female characters. In the week leading up to the Oscar presentations, one critic made the point that many actors could have played the autistic character in *Rain Man*, but that Dustin Hoffman was probably the only major star courageous enough to tackle such a complex and demanding role. Present-day male movie stars seem obsessed with their screen personae and utterly preoccupied with how they are presented to the public. Given the choice, the overwhelming majority would rather play dashing racing-car drivers or crusading law-enforcers than mentally handicapped loners. From the birth of cinema, female actors have been equally as conscious of the importance of image. Prior to the advent of the liberal eighties and nineties, all that was required of most was that they should look decorative and play a peripheral role. Those days have deservedly gone; women presented in films have ceased to be wilting damsels in distress and, in many cases, have become heroes themselves. The characters played by the five nominees in 1989 were a towering indication of how substantial this welcome change has been. At last women were beginning to play a more credible and significant part on screen: a far cry from the dearth of female acting opportunities in the late seventies.

Why the enormous change in such a comparatively short space of time? Perhaps Hollywood's gradual move away from formulaic, brainless action movies towards quality drama for discerning adult audiences has led to better roles for women. Or has the industry been forced into this position because today's leading men, the Fords, De Niros and Gibsons, are getting older? There is now a crop of strong and brilliant women more than capable of taking over from the men. One must not forget that society itself has changed thanks to the persistence of campaigns for equal rights. Women have fought hard against the concept that looks come first. There are more first-rate female actors in Hollywood today than ever before. Their acting is perceptibly more accomplished and realistic than it was in the days of Grace Kelly, Ava Gardner, and Elizabeth Taylor. The emergence of such accomplished female performers as Sigourney Weaver, Meryl Streep, Glenn Close, Debra Winger and others has brought a fresh dimension to American cinema. Scriptwriters and the studios, although slow at first, eventually began to make fine use of their various talents, bringing a new depth of characterization to female roles. The advancement of women in modern society has been admirably reflected in Hollywood's recognition that there are other types of women apart from prostitutes, girlfriends, nurses, and secretaries. Casting directors are giving actresses parts that a decade ago might only have been written for men. Today's actresses routinely play a wide range of roles, including lawyers, cops, and journalists.

The archetypal new, liberated woman is Sigourney Weaver, who foreshadowed the advent of strong female acting talent with her role in *Alien* (1979). The sole surviving crew member of the starship *Nostromo*, she single-handedly defeats a fearsome extraterrestrial, after all the macho men have been systematically killed. She went on to carve out a career appearing as a modern heroine in a succession of 'women of the eighties' roles, and was just as much a feminist pace-setter at the end of the decade. In *Gorillas in the Mist* she was perfectly cast as a kind of one-woman conservation movement, saving the mighty mountain gorillas of Africa from near-extinction.

At six feet tall, Sigourney Weaver is far removed from traditional images of feminine perfection, epitomized by past stars like Monroe and Bardot. Even so her striking looks have been celebrated by photographers of the calibre of Helmut Newton, and paraded in fashion spreads for magazines such as *Vogue* and *Harper's Bazaar*. She has, some would say, a host of natural assets: an intelligent, sculptured face, accentuated cheekbones, a wide forehead and a long neck.

Her hair is brown and naturally curly, her eyes piercing and dark. A critic once remarked that Sigourney possessed 'the looks of an untouchable princess'. Certainly, there is something vaguely European about her appearance. Her mother is English.

On the threshold of middle age Sigourney's looks and figure remain wonderfully lean and trim, thanks to a strict regime of daily exercise. The pursuit of fitness is essential for her own well-being and peace of mind. 'When I can't go to the gym I feel awful.' She has always been the sporting type. Athletics, horse-riding and snorkelling, which she mastered during a long vacation in the Bahamas shortly after completing her role in *Alien*, are just a few of the demanding activities in which she indulges. The actress also enjoys dancing (as a child she was made to attend ballroom dancing lessons), and for an evening's entertainment prefers a trip to the theatre than a seat in the stalls of a movie house. Reading is another pleasure and she numbers Kingsley Amis' *Lucky Jim* among her favourite novels. She also enjoys poetry, especially that of Robert Frost and Shakespeare.

Sigourney Weaver is one of the most popular and acclaimed actresses in the world cinema, a genuine star in a firmament littered with pretenders. Rightly regarded as a performer of rare quality, who imbues her characters with a strong moral code, a welcome streak of feminine intelligence and, above all, credibility, her monumental rise to stardom in the eighties has been a long, hard climb. She has overcome what many people in the industry considered grave handicaps: her extreme height, prejudice towards her beauty and sex, and absurd preconceptions about her background and class. Yet all the while she has remained true to herself, close to her roots. She is today as personable as she has ever been: delightfully forthcoming, surprisingly approachable and diverting (in complete contrast to her intense and serious screen image), and remarkably uncorrupted. Fame has not changed Sigourney Weaver. She remains an unlikely star in a business where inflated egos and double-dealing are the norm.

1 *Sweet, Stupid Little Child*

Around the turn of the century Los Angeles was hardly the teeming metropolis that it is today. To the west lay great stretches of rustling, untroubled bean fields and orange groves all the way to the Pacific Ocean. There was also much fallow land and many farms, whose precious acres were used for fruit growing and livestock raising. But, as the city flourished after the advent of the railroads in the late 1800s, most of those who lived on the land were forced to yield to progress. Sigourney Weaver's grandfather was an easterner who had packed his bags, along with his dreams, and travelled to the west coast to try his luck. Many of California's early settlers were gold prospectors, but Sylvester Weaver Senr. was a shrewd businessman, full of ideas and foresight. He recognized the futility of looking for gold in the hills and instead steered his considerable talents towards the construction business which he knew would become a boom industry once the city began to expand. 'My father's family was rich for a while,' Sigourney told *Interview* magazine in July 1988. 'My grandfather was the president of the Chamber of Commerce in Los Angeles. But he sold his roofing company too early, or something like that, and then they didn't have any money.' Sylvester's wife was raised in Ohio, and was a quite remarkable woman, gifted and creative, the perfect foil for her entrepreneurial husband. She adored classical music and could play a variety of instruments. She also read the most cultured of literary works, wrote poetry and composed operas.

Sigourney's father was born in 1908, one of four children. He had a brother and two sisters. Thanks to the family fortune Sylvester Weaver Jnr. enjoyed a privileged childhood and the best education. By his grammar school years

Sylvester had mastered the game of chess, published his own news journal, the *Eagle*, and digested the rudiments of the building trade. He had also inherited his father's boundless energy and head for business, along with his mother's artistic leanings. At high school Sylvester displayed admirable proficiency at field sports; he was almost unbeatable at tennis, and was a welcome addition to any of the school's baseball teams. He won a reputation as a ladies' man, a sleek charmer who required little encouragement to show off his adroitness at either the Charleston or the fox-trot. As the roaring twenties drew to a close Sylvester wasted no time in tasting the last fruits of what was to become a lamented decade. The young Weaver assumed the guise of an impulsive playboy and man-about-town and was seen at all the big LA social functions and parties, usually in glamorous company. He was known to have dated Joan Crawford and Loretta Young.

After graduating from Dartmouth College, where he had majored in philosophy, Sylvester spent the whole of 1930 trekking around Europe and the Middle East living the life of an adventurer. The America which greeted him on his return was in the clutches of depression. The Wall Street crash had caused mass unemployment and millions of hapless citizens suddenly found themselves living on the poverty line. It was the era of 'Buddy, can you spare a dime?' Luckily Sylvester, with his wealthy background and academic prestige, found little difficulty in acquiring suitable employment. He initially worked as an advertising copywriter in Los Angeles. As his interest in that field soon weakened, he shifted to radio programme production with the CBS corporation, where his gift for new ideas was put to more creative use. In 1935 fatigue set in once again and so he searched for more stimulating ground on which to work. Moving to New York he produced *The Fred Allen Show* for the powerful Young and Rubicam ad agency. So great was his inspired input that within a year he had become manager of their radio department. In 1938 Sylvester drifted back into advertising, joining the American Tobacco Company. But he was and always would be a wanderer, easily bored with a position once all avenues had been satisfactorily explored. Once more on the move, Sylvester joined forces with his old Dartmouth classmate Nelson Rockefeller and together they beamed American propaganda to Latin America by way of the radio.

For a number of years Sylvester had enjoyed the status and benefits of bachelorhood. As middle age approached, he sensed that now was perhaps the best time for him to settle down. Career-wise, he was a success, although he had yet to leave his mark on any one single industry. It was his personal life that was in need of stability and responsibility. One evening, quite unexpectedly, he met and fell in love with a beautiful, dark-haired English actress called Elizabeth Inglis. They were introduced to one another at a party and, within six months, were married. The young and ambitious actress was in New York on tour with Patrick Hamilton's melodrama, *Gas Light*. During the play's popular run at London's Apollo Theatre in the early months of 1939 Elizabeth had made quite a name for herself playing Nancy, a churlish maid. She even managed to catch the ever-critical eye of the *Daily Telegraph*'s reviewer, who called her portrayal, 'a brilliant little study'. This was Elizabeth's first trip to the States and the prospect of acting on Broadway filled her with a sense of expectation. Before *Gas Light's* opening night she agreed to appear in another play, *Anne of England*, opposite Jessica Tandy. The show was a disaster and closed within a few weeks. Unfortunately, because of Equity regulations, which stated that an English actress working in America could only perform in one show every six months, Elizabeth was prevented from rejoining the cast of *Gas Light*.

Elizabeth's American visit wasn't entirely a wasted venture. Sylvester Weaver amply compensated for her botched Broadway début. Elizabeth was so enraptured by the man's charm and debonair manner that she freely gave up her career and homeland to marry him. Looking at the couple one might have supposed that they shared little in common, apart from their joint creative flair. But in her youth Elizabeth had been a keen athlete also. At the age of sixteen she qualified for the Wimbledon Lawn Tennis Championships. Alas, her father, who was a lawyer, but far from wealthy, refused to allow her to participate. 'My kids aren't going to play these rich people's games,' he lectured, 'because they're going to have to go out and make a living.' As she had grown into a young woman, Elizabeth's passion for sports had matured into a profound and lasting love for the theatre. She now courted ambitions to be an actress and won a place at the Royal Academy of Dramatic Arts, where she attended the same class as Vivien Leigh. A full list of Elizabeth's film appearances is not available. As her superstar daughter confesses, 'She won't even tell me the names of all of them.' Most of Elizabeth's British films, it seems, were minor works and her roles in them were minimal. She played only small roles in *Museum Mystery, Landslide*, and *Thunder in the City* (with Edward G. Robinson and Ralph Richardson), all made in 1937. Her two best known movies are Alfred Hitchcock's classic *The 39 Steps* (1935), where she plays Hilary, the daughter of the villain played by Godfrey Tearle (she appeared fleetingly during a party scene); and *The Letter* (1940), with Bette Davis, in which her name was changed by the studio to the very English-sounding Elizabeth Earl. 'It's fun to see a parent on TV, jumping around in old movies,' Sigourney told the *Sunday Express Magazine* in 1984. 'I think I'd notice her even if she weren't my mother.'

After the war, which saw Sylvester Weaver as a lieutenant in the Navy, the couple's dreams of starting a family were realized with the birth of a son, Trajan, named after Sylvester's favourite Roman emperor. So great was Sylvester's penchant for Roman history that he even considered calling Sigourney 'Flavia'. The arrival of Trajan marked the end of Elizabeth's acting career. Her desire to reach the pinnacle of her profession gave way to motherhood and family life. Sylvester's career, however, was on the verge of greatness.

Television arrived in the United States accompanied by the hopes and dreams appropriate to a new medium. Although it took a while to catch on with the American public, watching television eventually overtook cinemagoing to become the country's favourite recreational activity. The power and scope of TV was awesome. More people would see a televised production of *Hamlet* in one night than all the theatre audiences of history put together: a daunting concept. In this fledgling industry men of great vision arose. Arguably the most significant and remarkable, certainly the most innovative figure in television of the fifties, was Sylvester Weaver. In those early pioneer days the two great rival TV networks were CBS and NBC. Desperate to maintain their lead in the eternal war for ratings, NBC pressed hard to formulate fresh and exciting projects, and formats uniquely suited to live broadcasting. To this end, Sylvester Weaver was hired as director of programming in August 1949. For the young entrepreneur this was a golden opportunity to make his mark on a new and stimulating industry, one that was to change the face of the world.

Weaver's first major success at NBC was *Saturday Night Revue*, a variety extravaganza which premièred in late February 1950. *Your Show of Shows*, ninety minutes of madcap comedy live from New York, was the most ambitious and successful portion of the programme and made Sid Caesar a star while simultaneously launching the careers of numerous unknown writers, including Neil Simon and Mel Brooks. *Your Show of Shows* ran on NBC for five years and was wisely taken off the air at the zenith of its popularity. The very last edition featured a guest appearance by Sylvester Weaver himself.

The maestro's next brainstorm was undoubtedly his finest. *The Today Show*, a daily two-hour programme which mixed news items with self-help features and interviews, was broadcast live each morning from the RCA exhibition hall in the Rockefeller centre. In Sylvester Weaver's own words it was 'a milestone in the social history of this country'. Capitalizing on the huge success of *Today*, Sylvester turned his attention next to that elusive period of the evening beyond prime-time where, like the early morning slot, TV programmers had hitherto feared to tread. At the station, no one but Weaver believed in the concept of a late-night talk show. But the public immediately warmed to the idea, and *The Tonight Show* soon became a national institution, particularly when presenter Johnny Carson took over the reins. The *Today* and *Tonight* shows were brilliantly conceived programmes, both of them ideally suited to live TV. All subsequent chat shows have more or less evolved from them. They are Sylvester Weaver's greatest legacy to television.

The enchanted, glamorous, extraordinary world that Sylvester Weaver inhabited was the everyday environment into which his daughter was born. Susan Alexandra Weaver (later Sigourney) first drew breath on 8 October 1949. She was born in New York, the city where she was to spend most of her childhood and many of her later years. Susan led what can only be described as the life of a little princess. She was a spoilt, pampered, and sheltered child who lived in a virtual bubble of guiltless bliss and unblemished contentment. The real world hardly ever got a look in. Nannies and maids tended to her every whim and TV studios were her playgrounds. Susan Weaver grew up in the rich areas of Manhattan where she knew only wealth and ease. This resulted in a certain amount of naïvety on her part. The young Susan suffered from the delusion that the life she led was a normal New York childhood. In her mind no one starved and everyone got whatever they wanted. Very rarely was the Weavers' precious little daughter exposed to the variety of life that most people experience and only on the odd occasion was she allowed to play in public parks with 'common' children. Normally companions from similarly privileged circumstances would be carefully picked out for her. Such an enclosed existence, out of the harmful reach of reality, left Susan Weaver with little or no genuine knowledge of how other children lived, kids deprived of the benefits that she took for granted. How could Susan even begin to comprehend the sorrow felt by a child denied a toy because of the financial restrictions of a loving parent? Whatever luxuries she desired were well within her father's means.

In the first ten years of Susan's life, the Weavers resided in thirty different households. As in the past, when Sylvester had changed his jobs, he would now move home, in an attempt to defy the onslaught of stagnation and boredom. Today Sigourney remembers the various apartments in which she lived by the names of the elevator men, who were always her best friends. Although the family were constantly shifting location (the perennial joke at NBC was that Sylvester moved when his flat needed cleaning), they continued to live in basically the same areas of New York: the costlier reaches of Manhattan's East Side and Long Island's north shore. The purpose behind Sylvester's desire to change his address endlessly was not only the vagabond spirit within him, but also his longtime love of the ocean. His years with the Navy had left in his heart a desire to be always near water; thus the family would move whenever a flat was found which offered him a better view of the Hudson River. 'It comforted him, I think, that patch of blue,' Sigourney recalls. These various apartments, were relatively grand. One such apartment, in Sutton Place, once belonged to Randolph Hearst's mistress Marion Davies, whose most private part reputedly inspired the now legendary name 'Rosebud' in *Citizen Kane*. Another, in Manhattan, had its own swimming-pool. At one time the family owned seven televisions and numerous radios, all of which would be placed in different rooms of the house. Every day several of these sets would be switched on, their dials tuned to various stations, filling the air with a strange mixture of entertainment. Under normal circumstances such a hellish cacophony would have driven a person to the edge of despair. For Sylvester this was an effective, if slightly unorthodox, way to keep track of what the rest of the industry was doing, to catch up on any new trends and developments, and thereby keep one step ahead of the competition.

The Weavers also owned a couple of country retreats far away from the clamour and hubbub of the racy city. One of these was situated in Maryland and was the first house Sigourney ever lived in. The large colonial building was part of a farm, but the actress has no clear recollections of the place. Only a handful of faded photographs, and a vague feeling that the family might have spent their summers in Maryland with Sylvester commuting to the Big Apple, prove that she was once there. Sigourney's earliest distinct memory is of an incident on another farm, this one in Sands Point, Long Island, a dreary and isolated place which consisted of nine acres of dilapidated buildings and one house. The only livestock the Weavers bothered to keep were a few scrawny chickens. One afternoon, during an aimless stroll, the young Sigourney tripped and cut her leg on some rusting chicken-wire. Whilst attending to the wound she thought to herself, 'One day I'm going to remember this.' It seems that, even at this tender age, Sigourney was already analysing and retaining knowledge about personal experiences for later use in her acting. Once during an EST (Erhard Seminar Training) seminar, as part of a psychological training programme the actress undertook in the late seventies and early eighties, she was encouraged to go back to her first memories. 'I did feel as though I was raging, trying to get attention, when I was coming into the world,' Sigourney recalled to *Interview* magazine in July 1988. 'Who knows if that was really a memory or just an instinct?'

The Schusters of Simon & Schuster, the noted American publishers, also lived at Sands Point in a beautiful mansion that overlooked the Atlantic, and were close friends and neighbours of the Weavers. Susan looked forward to her regular visits there with unconcealed delight and eagerness, for the sole reason that in one of the rooms Mrs Schuster kept a wide assortment of children's books to which she allowed the happy child complete and unrestricted access. This room became Susan's own private little grotto, a treasure-trove full of hidden delights and magical rides into a world of fantasy and adventure. This was a place where a talented child's keen imagination could run riot. Sometimes as a special treat Susan would be presented with a book which she could take home with her to read. Today Sigourney remembers Mrs Schuster as being 'like a fairy godmother', and has described her time at Sands Point as 'sort of my roots'. Her love of literature and fondness for books arose from those happy times, times which sadly now only exist as a series of disjointed memories. Today Sands Point has become a sorry dumping ground for asphalt.

To say that Susan Weaver grew up in show business surroundings would be a gross understatement. In December 1953 Sylvester became president of NBC. At the time the network was in organizational chaos. Several presidents had proved unsatisfactory and, out of all the in-house personnel, Sylvester Weaver was felt to have the right qualities for leadership and was awarded the presidency. He was now the undisputed king of television, a role in which he could truly help to influence the evolution of the medium. Under the guidance of Sylvester Weaver NBC grew in both stature and power. His amazing programming abilities and infectious enthusiasm generated a new air of excitement at the company. He was respected and revered by many of his associates, and his every utterance or communiqué was digested and analysed as if it contained the words of a prophet. His office meetings, in which the unorthodox executive would balance on an exercise device called a 'bongo board', became legend, as did many of his baffling verbal memos: 'I've been earring the ground'; 'The formula of the half-hour show is strictly handcuffs'; 'A fortuitous concatenation of circumstances'. During his brief tenure as NBC president Sylvester's willingness to innovate reached dramatic proportions when he embarked upon his biggest gamble yet, a series of TV specials (or 'spectaculars', as he called them), big budget shows with star name performers and elaborate sets. Another daring escapade was a personal crusade to raise the cultural standards of what Americans saw on television. Sylvester Weaver believed that prime-time TV should enrich and educate the audience as well as being a source of entertainment. His hope was to introduce ballet and the theatre into mainstream programming. Sadly, the gallant experiment failed; the mass populace seemed to prefer crime shows and westerns to his brand of highbrow entertainment.

As a young, impressionable child Susan was inevitably drawn into her father's world. To a large extent Sylvester's life was his work; the man did a great deal of his best thinking outside office hours. In this way, Susan became acquainted with what her father did and how he earned his living from an early age, even if she didn't quite comprehend all the complexities of his position until much later. Some of the biggest TV celebrities of the decade visited the Weaver household. Performers like Sid Caesar and Milton Berle, who to millions were just flickering monochrome images on the small screen, were part of Susan's everyday life, real people who would sometimes bounce the giggling girl on their famous knees: 'The people who came over to the house were wonderfully crazy.' One Christmas Susan was struck down with chicken-pox. No child enjoys being ill, especially during the festive season, and Susan Weaver was no exception. Wrapped up in bed, and feeling pretty miserable, Susan received an unexpected call from Art Linkletter, the popular host of the children's show *Houseparty*, who was soon able to cheer up the sorrowful youngster. One encounter with an NBC star, however, was far from amusing. J. Fred Muggs, the chimpanzee sidekick of *Today* host Dave Garroway, was a mischievous and bad tempered ape. When the two first met at the Rockefeller centre, when Susan was just six, she was assaulted by the animal and her new hat and dress were ripped, an attack which led to the monkey being barred from the Weavers' home. 'He was a vicious little beast,' she remembers. Susan's paternal uncle 'Doodles' Weaver was another well-known personality. He was the lovable clown in the Spike Jones band and appeared in a number of Bob Hope movies. 'Doodles' also took great pleasure in making Susan and her brother laugh.

Memories like these are precious and the young Sigourney Weaver had more than her fair share of happy times. Life was far from dull when Sylvester was around; he lived in near-constant fear of succumbing to tedium. The family benefited enormously from this unusual, if mild, state of neurosis: they had wonderfully orchestrated vacations and exciting new experiences. Susan, who sensed that her parents enjoyed themselves far more than their chic and rich friends, was often treated, with her brother, to big nights out at the theatre or cinema. Another advantage of having a father in the upper echelons of the television industry was that the family owned a gold ID card which allowed them behind the scenes at a host of hallowed studios, including the Radio City Music Hall. Susan and Trajan spent many happy hours exploring and playing in this vast and illustrious building. Full of dark hiding-places, whirring noises, manic activity and twinkling lights, the Radio City was the ultimate doll's-house, a giant play area of fun and learning. When Sylvester eventually lost all power at NBC it was a hard adjustment for his daughter Susan: no more golden passes.

Sigourney has carefully chosen the word 'peripatetic' to describe her parents. Due to their hectic life style, both Sylvester and Elizabeth took great delight in attending glitzy openings and parties and were well known socialites during his reign at NBC. She and Trajan were looked after principally by hired help, nannies and the like. This is not to say that their childhood was bare of parental love. The fact remains that, despite her elitist upbringing, the turmoil and upheaval of continually being on the move, and Sylvester's high-powered job and social ranking, Sigourney has grown up into a normal and well-adjusted woman. This is in complete contrast to some offspring of the rich and famous, who turn into miserable brats or egotists, or the sad few who find the strain too great and sink into the tragic world of alcohol and drug abuse: those who live fast and die young. As a child, Sigourney was amply protected from all external hostilities, the cruel outside world and the pressures of Sylvester's work hardly ever filtered through to harm her. His enormous self-confidence held the family together, even through the toughest times. The young Sigourney couldn't help but be guided by Sylvester's supreme faith in himself and his ideas, and by his attitude to life and business. Whereas many of us only see our parents lead normal lives and hold ordinary jobs Sigourney saw her father run one of the most powerful and important companies in America.

Brought up to believe that she was a special child, and in a different class to most other people, little Susan Weaver attended the best schools, took ballet lessons and was taught good manners, breeding and other qualities that befit a young lady, in addition to a deep-rooted feeling for high culture. Her mother, although retired from the stage, had lost none of her love for her craft and often exposed the children to the delights of the theatre and to classical music and the finest literature. Although Sigourney's decision to become an actress wasn't made until much later in life, one wonders just how much she was subconsciously shaped by her background. Sigourney disagrees with the theory that her show business upbringing dictated the pattern of her future existence. Yet she once conceded, 'In my family, show business was part of our world. I don't think I got a chance to see what something else would be like. I didn't mean to go into show business, but I think I naturally gravitated towards it.' Susan's parents, their friends and the surroundings in which she grew up almost certainly influenced her life profoundly. Susan Weaver was extremely intelligent for her age and, like a sponge, she couldn't help but absorb some of the showbiz atmosphere.

In a strange way, the innocent Susan equated the entertainment business with real life. To her, this perpetual merry-go-round of fun and happiness *was* the real world: 'I was so naïve that I thought everybody's father worked in television.' It was hardly surprising that she went on to crave a career that seemed so normal: this existence gave her so many marvellous gifts and happy memories.

In the mid-fifties, television and those who governed it were changing rapidly. The old guard was being rudely usurped by a new and power-thirsty breed of entrepreneurs. The biggest casualty was Sylvester Weaver. Despite his long list of impressive achievements at NBC and his years of loyal service, the fact remained that he had failed to win the ratings war with CBS. In the last year of his administration NBC had fallen dangerously behind their old rivals. The top brass was far from overjoyed with the network's recent performance and Sylvester paid the ultimate price. In December 1955 he was abruptly kicked upstairs to the post of chairman of the board. His new duties carried with them barely any control; the power to create and influence had been curtly wrenched from his once capable hands. He no longer had any say in the day-to-day running of the network. The proud and once great man could only tolerate the job for a few months. In September 1956 he resigned quietly and with the utmost discretion. NBC didn't even try to persuade him to stay; instead, they gave him a cash settlement of around $200,000 to make his move swift and painless. The money probably helped to ease the nagging guilt of those who had let him go, but it hardly alleviated the misery and disappointment that Sylvester must have felt. The company that he had helped to develop and grow had kicked him out into the cold. Sylvester Weaver's resignation sent shock waves through the entire industry. Of course, Sylvester was not wholly to blame for his fall from grace. To some extent he was the scapegoat for NBC's declining popularity. Other factors played their part, too. Television was now evolving at lightning speed, and an all-new hierarchy pushed hard to remove Sylvester's generation in order to forge ahead with more modern ideas. Sylvester had every right to feel angry about his treatment at the hands of NBC, and in later years he became a cynic and harsh critic of the industry he had once loved. As early as 1957 he referred to television as 'a jukebox to put in the corner to keep kids quiet': the words of a resentful and bitter man?

Sylvester Weaver's contribution to the early days of television is immeasurable. The late Goddard Lieberson called him 'probably the only true visionary who ever headed up a TV network – then or now'. The longevity of such programmes as *Today* and *Tonight* gives testimony to the true genius for programming that he gave to the infant medium. Sylvester, however, wasn't planning on taking early retirement: he was just forty-eight. In 1957 he dreamed of starting a fourth network channel, an immense enterprise which was doomed from the very outset. As a free agent and with a solid reputation behind him, Sylvester naturally assumed that other stations would be enthusiastic about employing him. Sadly, this was not to be the case. Was the whole thing a conspiracy to keep him out of power? Sigourney believes that there was an inordinate amount of jealousy and rivalry swelling up inside the industry and that the new bosses, wishing to preserve their own private dominion, were reluctant to hire this maverick genius. Sylvester never really worked in network television again. In the words of one family friend he became 'a prophet no one would listen to'.

The débâcle at NBC had a profound effect on the Weaver family, especially the children. From an early age, Susan and Trajan were under no illusions that a lot was expected of them; they were children with a special calling and had much to live up to. This was apparent in the names that Sylvester had bestowed upon them – (Susan) Alexandra and Trajan were imperial figures. The burden on brother and sister became heavier after Sylvester's fall from power in 1956. Trajan, the natural successor to his father's vision, declined the honour, dropped out and surfaced later as a committed Mormon, which left Susan with the job of redeeming Sylvester's dreams. This had a dramatic impact on her: she began wearing some of her brother's clothes in an effort to emulate him. Sigourney remembers being driven by what she calls 'daughter guilt'. But as Susan started to grow, her own sparkling personality began to surface and it soon became apparent that she had inherited many of the finer traits of her two highly gifted parents. A love of drama and the arts was Elizabeth's bequest to her daughter, while Sylvester instilled in Susan an appetite for success and an ambitious drive.

In contrast to most other girls of her age group Susan did not play with dolls and toys; she was already an avid academic and an eager bookworm. At grade school she read such diverse works as *Moby Dick* and *Suddenly Last*

Summer. Reading presented Susan with the opportunity of acting out her fantasies; in her imagination the characters from books were brought vividly to life. She was also maturing at a rapid speed. By the time Susan reached her teens she was a tall, intelligent and cultured young woman. The last two qualities helped her excel at some of New York's most celebrated schools. Susan first attended the Brearley Girls Academy, but Elizabeth moved her to another prominent establishment, Chapin, because she preferred the uniforms there. Susan's extreme height was initially an almighty hindrance at school. By the age of thirteen she was a lanky 5 feet 10 inches and a rather clumsy ugly duckling of a teenager. At Chapin, Susan became the centre of attention for all the wrong reasons and was constantly laughed at and made fun of by the other children. What often happens in such cases is that the tormented child deliberately accentuates her physical defects and accepts the role of class clown. This was certainly true in the case of Susan Weaver. It was during this period that she began to participate in school drama productions. Her very first stage role was Bottom in *A Midsummer Night's Dream*. Acting was a kind of release from the personal anguish she was currently enduring, although, to a certain degree, she was already putting on a performance by making her fellow school-mates laugh. Susan had discovered that acting, like reading, was a way in which she could create characters, and assume the identity of another person, mapping out their destiny and living out their experiences.

Meanwhile, Sylvester was finding out the hard way that doors open to him during his reign at NBC were now being firmly shut in his face. He was no longer attentively listened to by the people that mattered. All his new programme ideas seemed to fall on deaf ears. Sylvester soon grew tired of this constant rejection and eventually left New York to strike out afresh in California. Susan was just thirteen when the family packed their bags, uprooted, and moved the long distance to San Francisco. Here the revitalized Sylvester became a major force behind the first ever pay cable television system. STV, as it was called, planned to beam a wide variety of programmes into thousands of homes along the West Coast. Sylvester was hired as president and the station went on the air in July

1964. Weaver's expectations were justifiably high, but unfortunately STV was beset with problems from the beginning and failed to take off. There were certain factions, namely the theatre owners and the commercial broadcasters, who didn't want to see cable television flourish and proceeded to put STV out of business in a highly dubious manner. It was a nasty and bloody fight. Sigourney remembers death threats arriving on her father's doorstep.

For Susan, San Francisco was something of a culture shock, and her brief time in the city was less than congenial. In New York the teenager had been well protected from the harsh realities of everyday existence. This shielded upbringing had produced a shy and anxious girl who found herself unable to mingle with people her own age. She felt particularly lost amidst the fast-living inhabitants of an early sixties California, an open and relaxed society, relatively free of restrictive pressures, where different racial and cultural groups mixed readily. The class system which was seen as so important in New York just didn't exist on the West Coast: here you were accepted on your own merits as a human being and judged on recent achievements, not past glories. Your background, your parents' wealth and social standing, accounted for very little. Many of the Californian girls that Susan encountered on her travels shocked her greatly, they were so different from her friends back home in the Big Apple: 'I met girls who were twenty years older than I was who were my age.' Susan simply failed to embrace the youth scene in San Francisco. This generation's philosophy and outlook on life was completely at odds with her own. She failed even to relate to their interests, their taste in music and fashion. Boys were also a problem for the tall, shy and self-conscious teenager who describes herself then as an 'ugly duckling'. Suitable and willing male escorts were rare.

Susan's stay in California was thankfully short-lived. 'I wanted to go away to school. I had this romantic idea of what boarding-school would be like. Then I went away to Ethel Walker's where I just cried for the first year.' Ethel Walker was a private school of much propriety in Simsbury, Connecticut, and was populated largely by girls who came from privileged backgrounds. Susan's decision to attend boarding-school, the perfect escape route from an alien

California, can be interpreted as a desire to return to the warm familiarity of her childhood when she was cosseted and protected from the outside world. But the perceptive Susan was aware of a noticeable difference between herself and the average Ethel Walker pupil. Many of her new school colleagues were from extremely rich and powerful stock, whose massive fortunes were the product of old inheritances, whereas Susan knew that her father had made his fortune by going down to work at a television studio. 'We were like gypsies compared to those New England people.'

There was a justifiable feeling of expectancy amongst some of the students at Ethel Walker when the tall and seemingly athletic Susan Weaver attended her first class. The general consensus was that the school's new basketball star had arrived. Sure enough, Susan was ordered to participate in the sport, but she disliked basketball intensely, mainly because she wasn't very good, and was soon allowed to drop out. The sprightly teenager preferred to direct all spare energy into her dance classes. Ethel Walker were proud of their dance department and Susan enjoyed all her lessons there. 'My one regret, besides not learning science, is that I would have liked to have become a choreographer,' Sigourney later confided to *Interview* magazine in July 1988, 'I think that's a really interesting field. Not for musicals, but for modern dance.' That first year at Ethel Walker was an arduous one. By the end of term Susan's fellow school-mates had voted her 'Freshman Fink': 'the nerdiest girl in my class'. Hardly a boost to her flimsy confidence. Despite this initial setback, Susan managed to win a reputation for herself among the teaching staff as a top-class student, hard working and well mannered. She took to all her classes, English literature, algebra and history, well, and every night the eager pupil would most likely be engrossed in her beloved story-books or studying for the next day's lessons. Susan's height, however, was yet again causing problems and personal heartache. She still stood at least a head above most of her contemporaries and was forced to return to her role of class clown in order to win acceptance, perhaps even sympathy, and to shield off attack. 'I was very uncoordinated. A laughing stock.' She had also grown to despise her own name. Sick and tired of being called Sue or Suzie, names which were far too plain and better suited to little girls, she desperately wanted to find a replacement, something a bit more grandiose, a name befitting her personality.

One night, while reading F. Scott Fitzgerald's *The Great Gatsby*, Susan found the perfect new name. During a plush party scene, a flirting Jordan Baker asks Nick Carraway to contact her later under her aunt's name, Mrs Sigourney Howard. The name is mentioned only once and the aunt never actually appears, yet the impassioned reader was captivated by the sound and mystery that the word evoked. 'To my ear Sigourney was a stage name, long and curvy.' Sigourney is certainly an unusual name, the origins of which remain unknown, although it is close to the Eastern European root word for a gypsy, *zigganey*. The very next day Susan rounded up her best friends and announced that henceforth she was to be referred to as Sigourney. When her parents found out about the name change they were fairly upset and shocked; it had all happened so quickly and without warning. In the end they were most reasonable and respected their daughter's wishes, although Sylvester stressed the fact that in his opinion Sigourney was more of a man's name, and for a while both he and Elizabeth insisted on calling their daughter 'S', just in case she changed her name again. Sigourney was named after her mother's best friend in England, Susan Pretzlik, an explorer of some note and repute. Once, at a reflective moment, the actress confessed that if she had met Pretzlik before switching over to Sigourney she probably would have kept her original name. 'I think I'm very definitely a Suzie,' she later admitted to *Interview* magazine in July 1988. 'I wonder how perverse it would be if I had a daughter and named her Susan.'

During Sigourney's sophomore year at Ethel Walker her interest in the performing arts began in earnest. With a wonderful sense of enthusiasm and wild abandonment she threw herself into every conceivable school production. In one of her early plays, an adaptation of the poem *The Highwayman*, Sigourney was a motorcyclist dressed in a big leather jacket with her hair flipped back in mock-fifties Elvis style. 'We also did a whole Arabian sheik show,' she remembered fondly. 'I was the Valentino character.' In these school plays Sigourney was invariably cast in a male role due to her height and dark looks. After the humiliation of being tarnished with the dreaded handle of 'Freshman Fink', Sigourney fared slightly better in her second year and was promoted to 'Sophomore Fairy', an honour which entitled her to a little gold tiara and a broken wand which she would wave in the air as she sprinkled talcum-powder over bemused students heads on special occasions. In her third and final year Sigourney achieved perhaps the school's highest accolade, the rank of 'Junior Birdman', which meant she had been voted the funniest girl in school. The prize brought with it much prestige and glamour. There were to be no more silly games with wands and talcum powder. Now on those special school days, Sigourney's fellow students would carry her on their shoulders, crying in unison, 'Up in the air, Junior Birdman!' The humour that Sigourney had employed as a means of repelling ridicule and scornful taunts about her height had now won the talented academic a unique kind of popularity.

On the threshold of her departure from Ethel Walker Sigourney Weaver had little idea what the future would bring or what her role in life was to be. Her class-mates and friends seemed already to have their entire lives and careers clearly mapped out in front of them. They had specific plans and goals: some wanted to go into teaching, others wanted some kind of job in the arts. Like so many dreamers before her, the only thing Sigourney was really sure about was that she wanted to experience everything the world had to offer. Her ambitions were honourable, if perhaps a little too varied and wild. Sigourney used to change her career options like some people change their socks. She wanted to be a marine biologist, a doctor, a lawyer; she wanted to work with animals like Jane Goodall, who had successfully studied wild chimpanzees in Tanzania. Sigourney's teachers were at a loss as to how to make their student commit herself to one single, specific subject. In the end they pushed Sigourney towards a more concentrated study of English literature in the hope that her unique gift for bringing stories and fictional characters to life could be channelled into a teaching career. This was a wise move and, most importantly of all, Sigourney also appeared to like the idea.

During her summer breaks, Sigourney often stayed with

her parents at their plush home in Santa Monica. There she would feel compelled to play the devoted and submissive daughter and lead the life expected of a society girl, which entailed attending posh private functions and grand balls, not least her own glittering coming out party in November 1967. 'My parents just thought that in case Prince Charles was interested, I should have had every advantage.' Arguably the tallest débutante of the season, Sigourney still looked resplendent in her flowing white gown. It was clear for all to see that this particular ugly duckling had become a swan.

One memorable summer the Weaver family flew to Israel for a short vacation. Sigourney immediately fell in love with the country and sensed an affinity with the people. During a revealing interview with *Film Comment* in 1986 Sigourney confessed that she had once held a secret desire to convert to Judaism. 'I went to one of those schools where religion was a loose amorphous thing. If I'd married a Jew, I'm sure I would've converted.' Sigourney decided she wanted to stay on in Israel and work in a kibbutz. Her parents gave their permission and flew back to the United States. To the idealistic Sigourney, this seemed a chance to discover a new world, to find a utopian society where men and women were equal. Instead the young romantic was given the job of working a potato-peeling machine, which she succeeded in blowing up. Other reports suggest that her stay in Israel ended abruptly after she staged a one-woman strike, in protest at her permanent assignment as potato-peeler. Sigourney returned home after 'the most boring two months of my life'. The bruising experience left her dejected and miserable. Perhaps rather naïvely Sigourney had expected the kibbutz to be one long party because all her Jewish friends back at college were extremely good humoured and always used to make her laugh. 'But Israeli culture isn't the same as Jewish culture. The Israelis were all serious workers.'

At the age of sixteen, Sigourney won her first real theatre job working with a summer stock troupe in Southbury, Connecticut. 'It was a pretty strange life. We worked terribly hard.' Over the course of that summer Sigourney was cast in two productions at the Red Barn Playhouse. She played all the extra women, flower-vendors and the like in *A Streetcar Named Desire*, and was cast as Alice in *You Can't Take It*

With You. Alice was one of the play's main characters; it was a great role, a real challenge, and Sigourney couldn't wait to get to grips with the text. But there were problems. The producer had cast his boyfriend opposite Sigourney and then callously fired her because his lover was about half the actress's height. Sigourney was extremely hurt and offended by this incident. Almost immediately she was on the phone to her mother, pouring out her woes. Expecting to hear a sympathetic voice on the other end of the line, Sigourney instead received some carefully judged words of advice. 'Well, welcome to the business,' said Elizabeth. 'Your heart will be broken a hundred times.'

2 *Almost Grown*

The Stanford football stadium is a large and imposing building, one of the most important and well-attended leisure facilities in the attractive city of Palo Alto, California. On a mild afternoon in May 1969, the thousands of students from the nearby university united on the stands had not come to cheer on their favourite football team but to attend a huge and highly organized political rally, the emphasis of which, due to the hated conflict in Vietnam, was decidedly anti-war. Part of the entertainment consisted of a play called *Alice in ROTCland*, enacted by a 'guerilla' theatre group. The performance protested against the presence of ROTC (Reserve Officers Training Corps thousands of students a year graduate with commissions in the Officers Reserve Corps, after four years' training under regular army instructors as part of their college courses) on the campus grounds of Stanford University. The actors were all students who had entrusted Sigourney Weaver with the job of bringing to life the lead role through the use of her strong, but at the time rather raw and ingenuous, performing powers. The performance was held at an important juncture, signalling the beginning of a large demonstration against old-style imperialism creeping back into American foreign policy. For the most part, the play was ineffectual, a tired collection of acrimonious political rhetoric. Sigourney's hard work throughout went largely unnoticed by the assembled masses, except for one moment which provoked an unbelievable response in the crowd. The scene where Sigourney holds aloft a copy of *Chairman Mao's Sayings* (commonly known as Chairman Mao's *Little Red Book*) was the play's *coup de grâce* and the culmination of weeks of rehearsals and dedicated graft by all the participants.

Sigourney's preparation for her role was substantial. Not only had she purchased the red book especially for the occasion, but she had studied Mao's writings and sayings in detail. However, when the climactic moment arrived Sigourney discovered to her horror that she had forgotten to bring the book to the stadium. She began frantically searching through her haphazard belongings for the missing item. Alas, the book was nowhere to be found. With adrenalin and fear pumping through her body, and a thousand spectators watching and waiting, Sigourney improvised brilliantly, and with breathless speed she picked up and waved in the air her address book, filled with the names of her debutante friends. This one, simple action proved devastatingly effective, as hundreds of incited students stormed out of the stadium and set fire to the ROTC building at the university. Not surprisingly, the heads of the school were somewhat irked by the wilful destruction of their ROTC office, now a burnt ruin of smouldering wood and blackened stone. For weeks after the event Sigourney lived in near-constant fear of administrative reprisals: would she be arrested for fuelling a riot or, even worse, expelled from the college? As Sigourney waited for the dust to settle she was prone to bouts of paranoia and often refused to answer the phone or the door to her rooms. Luckily, the authorities decided against making a scapegoat of her. Meanwhile, on campus, she attained fleeting heroic status. The ROTC affair taught Sigourney Weaver a lasting lesson about the power of acting and how much influence a performer can have over an audience. 'Talk about theatre having an effect on people.'

In the late sixties, with America midway through one of the greatest social upheavals in its history, such a disturbing and anarchic incident as the destruction of a government building was commonplace. Young Americans were once again disillusioned; but, unlike the juvenile delinquents of the fifties, who used a superficial and manufactured form of rebellion, borrowed from James Dean, with which to attack their parents, this new generation had all but declared open warfare against the whole of established society. With each passing day, thousands of people were 'freaking out' and joining the multitudes who had already bypassed the road to normality and boldly struck out on their own. Communes and alternative living grew popular, as did the drug culture that was seen to be a principal part of such a life style. The late sixties were to become synonymous with hippies, sit-ins, LSD, and free love. Many saw California as the location of these influences. The peace movement and the naïve flower children largely emanated from San Francisco, the very city that the bewildered and disorientated teenager had run away from, unable to relate to the carefree life enjoyed by the younger residents of the West Coast. Then Sigourney had felt like an alien amongst people of her own age, an outcast. She had escaped to Connecticut where she embraced the strict and conformist life indigenous to boarding-school. But she had returned, a little older, a little wiser. In the interim, Sigourney Weaver had grown bored of the East Coast; now she longed to be free of the rigours and regulations of prep school, and the conventional world of débutante balls and private functions to which her parents had subjected her. Stanford University offered her the chance to leave such dreariness behind. Sigourney was now ready to join the swinging and spontaneous new world. On the threshold of higher education she still possessed mixed views about the sort of career she wanted. For a while Sigourney entertained thoughts about being a newspaper journalist, 'the curiosity is the same as an actor's,' and for a fleeting moment she contemplated applying for an internship on the *Washington Post*. In the end Sigourney decided to take her former teachers' advice and major in English with the hope of earning a Ph.D. and joining the honourable teaching profession.

Famous for its academic excellence, Stanford University is located in the north-west corner of Palo Alto, a charming city near San Francisco. Palo Alto is known today for its environmental policies and praised as one of the 'model little cities of the world'. It was the perfect institution for a bright and gifted student like Sigourney Weaver. (Before her move to Stanford Sigourney had entered Sarah Lawrence College, another top academic establishment, but dropped out within a year because she was 'tired of being sheltered by yet another school'.) In common with the laid-back and liberal mood then prevalent in the Bay Area, Stanford was nowhere near as stern or as authoritarian as some of the other universities. In fact, the faculty actively encouraged the students to express themselves openly and to exercise their right to be free and independent. Sigourney found the atmosphere at Stanford a healthy and most invigorating one. The university itself, although lacking the greenery associated with the Ivy League schools on the East Coast, was beautiful. Architecturally, Stanford's pleasant, rough-hewn sandstone buildings are Romanesque in styling, though the red-tiled roofs, the burnt adobe colour of the stone, and the wide arches give the university a Spanish mission look. These pleasant surroundings were certainly conducive to the learning process and Sigourney immediately fell in love with the place and began to impress her tutors with a succession of high marks.

Just before her move to Stanford, Sigourney found her mother an inspiration for her discovery of her own emerging beauty. This once ridiculed teenager now found looking into a mirror less the punishing duty it had once been. From an ugly duckling she had grown into a beauty-contest winner. At Stanford her bubbly personality and quick wit bewitched many, while her sculptured face and long legs attracted numerous male admirers. Sigourney enjoyed the attention she received, finding it a pleasant change from the snide stares and back-stabbing comments that had been customary at her previous schools. She began dating a select batch of favoured men. Her lofty stature, once a source of derision, was now a great asset. Even so, many considered Sigourney to be slightly out of step with the rest of the student body because of the way she conducted herself on campus. Just as during her childhood she had been occasionally prone to carry her reading over into real life, so it was now with her acting. However naïve such a thing may sound Sigourney still liked to assume the guise of characters from the latest book or play she had read. In the conservative and conformist 1990s such behaviour from a top-grade university student would give rise to serious questions about the individual's sanity! But the sixties was an era unto itself and such conduct would only have raised a few quizzical eyebrows and labelled its performer a slight eccentric. In an age when the new youth was stretching the boundaries of fashion, music and morals, and trying their damnedest to shock society and their elders, one quirky girl's silly way of living out her fantasies would seem unimportant. The relaxed atmosphere at Stanford allowed Sigourney such ample freedom of expression. Most importantly, Stanford presented her with an escape route from the shackles of her rich girl past. At no other time in recent history has an opportunity arisen for a student to leave behind the aura of prep school and the trappings of a privileged upbringing so easily. Today, Sigourney would most likely be shunted into a predetermined group with other graduates of a similar social ranking.

Despite the fact that Stanford didn't possess a very good drama department in the late sixties, Sigourney still managed to attend a few acting classes and join a local theatre group. In her second year the acting bug began to bite more intensely. Sigourney took part in two Shakespeare plays. She portrayed Ariel in *The Tempest* and Goneril in a 'rather irreverent' production of *King Lear*, which was presented in the form of a Japanese Noh play. Even this early on Sigourney was enjoying the thrill of experimenting with theatre styles and the structure and staging of plays, be they modern or classic. Her next step was to join a progressive band of young actors who can only be described as latter-day wandering minstrels, a bedraggled bunch who toured the Bay Area in a covered wagon. The idea was to stop somewhere, a park perhaps or some other open space, and perform commedia dell'arte theatre to whomever would stop and watch. What attracted Sigourney to this troupe's particular brand of drama was their heavy reliance on improvisation. Their whole approach to acting was refreshingly different, if a little dangerous for the performer. Because their theatre was spontaneous and encumbered by few rules one was always on the thin line between success or failure. Immediate reaction and a close rapport with the audience amply compensated for the odd duff performance. Sigourney had, to some extent, found her niche: this was the sort of acting that really appealed to her; she could instantly create her own characters and situations. Sigourney enjoyed, and learnt much from, the brief time she spent with the group.

Because of the great social issues of the time, civil rights and Vietnam, Sigourney was inevitably drawn into student politics. She became something of a political activist. The war in south-east Asia, the horrors of which were brought home to American people every night as they sat and watched television, had caused massive domestic unrest. While men, some of whom were the same age as the idealistic Sigourney, fought and died in Vietnam in a conflict they didn't understand, a different kind of battle raged on the campuses of America. Vietnam became the biggest and most crucial issue of the generation and Sigourney desperately wanted her voice to be heard just as loudly as those of her colleagues. 'Stanford was a good place to go to school then because the campus became radicalized about the war in Vietnam,' she remembers. Often Sigourney and her classmates would mingle with some of Stanford's more politically aware students. She decided to use acting as the platform from which she could then make her protests public. Consequently she joined a 'guerilla' theatre group. Sigourney's involvement with this gang of radicals, which was comprised mostly of the estranged offspring of the East Coast ruling class, hints at the possibility of an act of rebellion against her family background.

The late sixties and early seventies was the age of drug taking and Sylvester, quite naturally, was openly concerned for his daughter's welfare. His fear was that she had fallen in with the wrong crowd. He referred to Sigourney's new friends as her 'drug-fiend idiot classmates'. Sigourney soon put his mind to rest. 'I don't know what it is about me,' she confessed to *Première* magazine in October 1988. 'I can't seem to take drugs at all.' Sigourney's high has always been achieved on the stage.

The sole aim of the politically minded actors was to make audiences aware of current issues and topical problems through plays and sketches. In the main, the group were called upon to provide the entertainment at rallies, such as the one at the Stanford football stadium. 'We would be the jesters,' Sigourney told *New York* magazine in June 1984. 'Most of what we did would be funny. At that point I wasn't going to be an actor.' One of the troupe's prime objects of protest was the Stanford Research Institute. This was where napalm was invented and where other hideous chemical-warfare research took place. The institute was situated right next to the university building, a precarious location given the anti-war mood among the student fraternity at the time.

Ronald Reagan, then governor of California, often had to resort to sending in the National Guard to quell student uprisings, convinced in his own mind that they were orchestrated by Communists. Sigourney and her co-protesters took perverse pleasure in watching the soldiers 'invariably tear gas those apolitical middle-class students in the dorm playing bridge'.

Sigourney Weaver's interest in political theatre slowly evaporated towards the end of her stay at Stanford. From the very real world of rallies and anti-war parades Sigourney took up residence in what can only be described as a semi-fantasy world. In her last term at university she moved into a tree house with a male friend and began to dress like an elf. She had built her new open-air abode herself. This was no great architectural feat: the dwelling was rather crudely constructed. 'It didn't take a lot of skill.' Dismissed by many at the time as a silly fad, the tree house was a necessity. Sigourney simply couldn't find anywhere to live and had no intention of remaining in a dorm. Her actions were not really that unusual when taken in the context of the era and the community to which she belonged. Many of her friends, for instance, lived a basic and communal existence in domes and tents up in the hills outside San Francisco. But dressing up in a home-made elf costume was a touch bizarre. Sigourney and her companion wore matching outfits in a wide variety of bright colours. As they strolled gaily together across campus no one could fail to notice them. They were a strangely hypnotic couple who attracted interested stares from both hostile and admiring eyes with their beguiling beauty. 'It wasn't as if I were this astounding eccentric. Everyone I knew was strange,' Sigourney told *You* magazine in November 1989 whilst in reflective mood about those dim and distant times and perhaps feeling duty-bound to defend them. Her parents, on the other hand, didn't quite see it like that. Not only was their daughter living with a man out of wedlock (hardly a rare occurrence among students), but she was living an almost wild existence up a tree, eating vegetables procured from the university's own research gardens. (One wonders how much of Sigourney's free spirit antics and eccentric behaviour at Stanford, which were legacies from her father, represented a reaction against her family and her own upper-class roots.) Despite Sigourney's behaviour, Sylvester and Elizabeth were pleased with her academic progress at Stanford. She had continued to study as hard as ever in the English honours programme and still seemed hell-bent on pursuing her Ph.D. However, serious doubts about whether she had made the right decision lurked beneath her sincere ambition to achieve that Ph.D. In her final term her lessons had grown dry and boring and Sigourney was worried that if the course continued in this fashion she wouldn't be able to cope with the sheer drudgery of it all. 'I was studying criticism of criticism.' In a state of mild turmoil Sigourney sought professional advice and was told by a teacher that, if anything, the lessons would get even more dull and tedious as the course progressed. That was the final straw: she was out.

This decision coincided neatly with a strong dream of Sigourney's. Despite the fact that she had never seriously studied acting at school nor been a drama major, the theatre had always held a special place in her heart and in recent years this passion had begun to consume her. She decided to leave Stanford and apply for a place at the Yale School of Drama. Her parents were only moderately pleased when they heard the news. Both had grave misgivings about seeing their daughter enter the acting profession, but were aware of Yale's glittering reputation as a respected seat of learning. In recent times Sylvester and Elizabeth had begun to notice that drama was becoming more than a mere after-college activity for their daughter. Veterans of the business, the Weavers never directly encouraged Sigourney to take to the stage. Both were familiar with the pain of failure and the distress caused by having one's talents and ideas constantly on trial and open to criticism. The heartbreak of rejection is a feeling an actor never quite recovers from and the Weavers were worried that their daughter was too shy and fragile even to survive the hostile world of show business, let alone to rise above it and succeed. Their greatest fear was that the industry would swallow her up. But once Sigourney declared her intentions to become an actress they both did all they could to help, while secretly still living in hope that one day she would see sense and settle down into some job this side of normality. Some friends and former teachers shared similar views. Prior to the Yale move they all tried desperately to persuade her to change her mind. Acting was such a risky business; only a select minority found true success.

Once reconciled to their daughter's decision, the Weavers offered her all the advice they could, plus the odd cautionary tale about the profession. The one thing they could not present Sigourney with was any kind of short-cut to the top. Even if her parents' old showbiz connections had been able to open doors for Sigourney one wonders if she would have taken advantage of the opportunity, given her independent nature. Even in her early days as a struggling actor in New York Sigourney was reluctant to trade on the family's once hallowed name. 'I had a horror of it.' However, Sylvester did present his daughter with a short list of people to call once she reached the Big Apple, former colleagues and associates of the great man who might be able to help her. Sigourney soon realized the futility of such a list when the first person she called suggested that she got a job working as a shop assistant in Bloomingdales. It was patently clear that if Sigourney was going to reach the top it would be by her own efforts and talents.

For her audition piece at Yale Sigourney chose a speech from *St Joan of the Stockyards* by Bertolt Brecht. One can only imagine what the expressions and the thoughts of the adjudicators must have been when they saw the elf-like Sigourney walk through their door in corduroy trousers, with a length of rope acting as a belt. But that was the least of her problems. The piece which she was about to perform in front of this rather stern-looking panel of teachers was woefully under-rehearsed. Attending auditions on the spur of the moment was a curious habit of Sigourney's in the early seventies. Before Yale she had auditioned for Lloyd Richards at NYU (New York University, situated in the heart of trendy Greenwich Village), who coincidentally went on to become the director of Yale's repertory theatre in the late eighties. Sigourney hadn't applied for a place at the school, she just strolled in from the street one day and belted out a Janis Joplin standard, much to the bemused amazement of Mr Richards who was so impressed with her boldness and ability that he offered the actress a place at the university. In a momentary lapse Sigourney declined it. But the Yale audition was an altogether different and more crucial affair, one which could determine the course of her future life. This was the academy that Sigourney had set her heart on attending and so it was important that she made a good first impression, especially if she was at all serious about pursuing a career in the arts. That Sigourney had allowed herself to arrive so poorly prepared showed either severe recklessness or supreme confidence. When the news filtered through that she had been accepted by Yale Sigourney probably registered little surprise; after all, her academic record and background spoke volumes. But she was still very lucky to have been chosen. Yale was very selective (up until 1969 only men were allowed to study there), and was among the country's most highly rated schools in terms of academic and social prestige. But there was one slight error in her letter of admittance. It was addressed to a Mr Sigourney Weaver. This clerical slip was only the first of what was to be a long series of misunderstandings between Yale and Sigourney.

As the weeks in California passed, following her graduation from Stanford Sigourney took full advantage of spare time prior to the big move to Yale to form her own drama group. This new company of eager young thespians chiefly performed outdoors in the parks of Los Angeles. For a while, Sigourney thought about trying to get a grant to start up her own proper theatre company. Although this endeavour served as an adequate way of keeping Sigourney's acting muscles in trim, the experience was too similar to her previous open-air drama outings to serve any real or measurable artistic purpose.

Situated in New Haven, Connecticut, a mere fifty miles from Simsbury, where Sigourney had studied at Ethel Walker, Yale is one of the oldest universities in America, dating back to the eighteenth century. Renowned for its libraries and museums, the university comprises twelve schools, including law, medicine, fine arts, music, and drama (which opened as recently as 1955). Like Stanford, Yale was a charming place in which to study. Beautiful gothic architecture, reminiscent of and perhaps inspired by Oxford and Cambridge, is a feature of the college, as are the splendid campus grounds. The newcomer had barely had time to settle in when disaster struck. Sigourney's second morning at the school was taken up by the boring and arduous inauguration of her fellow new pupils, after which she was acutely in need of some refreshment. She went to a delicatessen which was the local lunch-time haunt of those students who took a serious interest in what went into their stomachs. Sigourney tended to agree with the sound notion of healthy eating and ordered liver for lunch that afternoon. As she strolled down Chapel Street later she stopped hesitantly next to a shop-window cracked like a spider's web due to a big bullet hole, an ominous image that has stuck in her mind ever since. Sigourney suddenly felt a sickening tightening in her stomach, followed by a dart of pain. She had food poisoning and was rushed to hospital.

Once recovered, Sigourney prepared herself for the three year stay at Yale. She was excited by the prospect of attending what may have been the country's leading drama institution, and eager to tackle the variety of challenging roles she would be called upon to play. Her dreams were to be dashed in the cruellest way. Yale was not to be the great learning experience she had hoped for, but a punishing lesson in rejection and perseverance. To begin with, the way in which Yale taught drama was very different from the method applied by Stanford. The theatre that Sigourney loved was spontaneous and informal. At Yale this was frowned upon; their approach to acting was predominantly academic, much more serious and highbrow. (The Yale theatre programme was then run by Robert Brustein, who was very much an advocate of intellectual drama.) The plays of Shakespeare, Shaw and Chekhov were held in reverence by the average Yale student, whereas at Stanford Sigourney had been used to tackling even the most venerated of works with wild abandon in an effort to stretch her acting capabilities. 'Nobody ever said, "Well *Hamlet* is beyond us at this point, we're not experienced enough to understand Kafka," ' she said to a reporter from *New York* magazine in June 1984. 'We just did anything and had such a good time.' Sigourney's wonderful craziness manifested itself in some pretty off-the-wall drama work at Yale, similar in content to the kind of stuff she had been doing at Stanford. But this didn't go down very well with her new teachers and as a result Sigourney was harshly criticized. 'It took me a long time to realize that I wasn't wrong, they were.'

The first two years at Yale were a testing time for Sigourney; never before in her life had she felt such genuine misery and frustration. The most immediate problem to overcome was the fact that the teachers had categorized Weaver as 'uncastable', mainly due to her height. Sigourney was taller than the average male student and because of a nonsensical theatrical ruling that the man should always be taller than his leading lady, she was never given the opportunity to shine in a major role. Her emerging beauty was also considered to be a handicap. An actress unfortunate enough to possess film star good looks was deemed by the more serious-minded drama scholar to be of an inferior breed, 'an airhead'. Instead of the demanding roles that Sigourney had expected to play at Yale she more often than not portrayed minor characters, such as old ladies or prostitutes, characters that carried with them few challenging or educative qualities. To add insult to injury Sigourney wasn't even allowed the chance to prove that she was a capable actress because the students were prohibited from auditioning for any of the parts in forthcoming Yale productions. This was a ludicrous state of affairs for such a renowned drama academy; after all, a struggling actor spends most of his or her professional life attending auditions. Preparing students and teaching them how best to handle auditions, terrifying affairs at the best of times, should be an important part of a drama school's curriculum. Although Sigourney appreciated the wide variety of teachers on offer at Yale, she sometimes wished that she could have had the kind of educational experience that a lot of her English friends enjoyed at the Central School of Drama in London, where female students earned leading roles through talent and merit and where every aspect of the theatre was tackled. Sigourney never got the chance to study the works of such great American dramatists as Tennessee Williams, Eugene O'Neill and others because Robert Brustein had an aversion to them. At Yale, in a world of their own, the teachers simply dictated which student was to play which part. Meryl Streep, who was a year behind Sigourney, walked away with all the plum female roles. To say Sigourney was bitter would be an understatement. She felt anger and resentment that the school could charge such exorbitant fees for their courses and then cast only a select minority of students in all the top roles. In Sigourney's case, during the whole of her three years at Yale the teachers never once selected her for a leading part. 'There was so much hypocrisy and pettiness there,' she recalls.

Meryl Streep was the undisputed golden girl of Yale. She was idolized and envied by most of the students. Her potential genius for acting was there for all to see. Though Sigourney's work couldn't be more different from Streep's operatic interpretation of method acting, the two stars share an aura of aristocracy (they were born within a year of one another into rich families), an impeccable academic pedigree, (Sigourney studied at Stanford while Streep attended the equally illustrious Vassar and Dartmouth), and a mild disdain for Hollywood and the superficial trappings of stardom. A legacy of Yale perhaps or simply the result of entering showbusiness as adults rather than as gullible adolescents.

Both actresses also made strong reputations for themselves on the New York stage and today share the same agent. 'I think I get sent the roles that Meryl's not doing,' was one of Sigourney's perennial jokes of the mid eighties. Curiously their subsequent cinematic careers have not run on parallel lines. Streep, particularly at the dawn of her career, took on a profusion of weighty roles in heavy, dramatic projects such as *The French Lieutenant's Woman* and *Sophie's Choice*, while Sigourney, although a serious actress in her own right, made her name in fantasy movies zapping aliens and dodging ghosts.

But whereas Meryl was treated almost reverently by the Yale teaching staff, Sigourney was callously dealt with. Her tutors actively discouraged her from continuing as an actress. In their opinion she had no talent whatsoever and shouldn't even be contemplating a theatrical career. Meryl had waltzed in and become the school star, while Sigourney went unappreciated and overlooked. She was heartbroken when she was told that she had no future as an actress, because she assumed that these educated and learned men knew what they were talking about. This forced lack of confidence in her own abilities resulted in a long period of self-doubt. She began to believe the lie that she was wasting her time at Yale. These misgivings resulted in a dramatic physical change. Her natural beauty temporarily went out of the window, as did her wonderful and unique dress sense. She began to wear shapeless clothes which made her look dumpy and slightly overweight. Her slovenly appearance so angered the faculty that one contingent sought to have her expelled on the grounds that she displayed 'poor self-image'. Her saviour was Alvin Epstein, one of the drama directors, who defended the actress by arguing at a meeting of fellow tutors, 'You don't get rid of a Greek goddess just because she doesn't dress well'. Later some of the teachers who had down-trodden Sigourney were fired. This only served to confuse the poor girl even more.

To this day, Sigourney remains unsure about what exactly the Yale faculty wanted from her. 'I still think they probably had this Platonic ideal of a leading lady that I have never been able to live up to. And would never want to,' she disclosed to *Interview* magazine in 1988. Yale had dismissed Sigourney out of hand merely because they couldn't mould her into the kind of carbon-copy, conveyor-belt actress they wanted. They had completely failed to understand her. Sigourney never realized that this was because she was different from the rest, too much of a free spirit, and that this difference would eventually work for her, catapulting her to screen stardom. Sigourney disagreed vehemently with much of Yale's teaching philosophy. She willingly concedes the fact that show business is a ruthless way to make a living (her father always referred to the entertainment trade as 'the racket'), and not everyone is going to survive, but does feel that the staff at Yale were sometimes too tough on their students. They cruelly weeded out the weaker pupils so that by the end only the strong remained, battle-hardened for the rough and tough outside world of professional theatre. Sigourney wasn't the only victim. Whether this almost military practice was deliberate school policy is debatable. Sigourney herself believed that the individual should have the right to decide for themselves whether they wished to continue or not. 'I really don't think it was a responsible way to teach,' she told *Woman Journal* in December 1988. 'I think it's irresponsible of teachers to dismiss people out of hand just because *they* don't happen to respond to them.' Too often she saw talented people so discouraged by their tutors that they simply gave up, a predicament in which Sigourney almost found herself. It is to her credit that she remained at Yale despite all the pressures that were mounting up around her. 'I think the valuable thing for me was that I did stick it out somehow.' What Yale did do, however, was slowly but surely rob the ambitious Sigourney of all her passion and love for the theatre.

One aspect of Yale that did find favour with the budding young actress was the film school, which stood apart from the drama department. The course there turned out to be one of the most beneficial that she was to take at Yale. Two of the film teachers were actually noted cinema directors, steeped in critical and commercial glory – Arthur Penn (*Bonnie and Clyde*) and George Roy Hill (*Butch Cassidy and the Sundance Kid, The Sting*). In one lesson the students were asked to re-enact dramatic moments from the films, *Woyzeck* and *The Trial*. The class would work on each separate scene for a few hours. During that time each scene would be acted out in five completely different ways, sometimes faithfully, but mostly the dialogue would be changed and the students encouraged to improvise openly. The freedom of being able to change the text of a movie or play and the spontaneity and craziness of the classes must have been the elements that attracted Weaver to the film course. But when the drama department discovered that Sigourney was secretly attending the school she was banned from ever stepping foot in there again. 'They were very open-minded, weren't they?'

By her third year Sigourney had all but given up on the drama people and had begun making regular visits to the play-writing department. The writer's workshop was a weekly class in which drama students were invited to come along and read extracts from the student playwright's work: a most beneficial exercise for actors and writers alike. Such lessons gave Sigourney a big advantage over students in other drama schools. Here she got used to working with budding playwrights and dealing with new plays, which for an actor starting a career is where all the work is. At these classes Sigourney came into contact with some of the most talented and creative individuals she had ever known. Compared to her stuffy and pretentious drama colleagues these Bohemian writers were a breath of fresh air. Sigourney was thrilled to discover that these artists were also interested in experimenting, and extending the boundaries of contemporary theatre. But, most importantly, they were open to the actress and her wacky ideas. During her last tormented year at Yale the playwrights became her salvation; in their company she could relax, liberate her frustrations, and let off steam. Sigourney quickly made a number of friends in this coterie of wild artistic talent, many of whom went on to carve reputations for themselves on the New York theatre circuit – Albert Innaurato, Kate Macgregor-Stewart and Wendy Wasserstein, who was particularly struck by her acting. 'You would always notice Sigourney,' she said. 'Your eyes would always go to her.' Significantly the writer who was most impressed by Sigourney Weaver was Christopher Durang. 'She was the immediate star of her class,' he told *Interview Magazine* in July 1988. 'Beautiful, sculptured face, slender body – and she seemed to be about seven feet tall. She looked like a mythological goddess.' The first time Durang laid eyes on her she was wearing a costume that was comparable to her old Stanford elf garb. The sight of this tall and striking WASP wearing green pyjama pants with small dangling pompoms on the side of her legs, could have put Durang off her for life. The first time they actually spoke to one another turned out to be a rather unfortunate and dark occasion. Sigourney asked him, quite innocently, whether he had any brothers or sisters. Unbeknown to her, Durang's mother had been Rh-negative (a very rare and tragic blood disorder which causes a woman to give birth to still-born children). Durang politely answered the question. 'Yes I have three, but they're all dead.' There was complete silence, Sigourney stared at him in utter disbelief. Then she looked deeper into his eyes, realized that he was actually telling the truth, and roared with laughter. Lesser mortals, devoid of Durang's warped sense of the bizarre, might have reacted violently, but he saw the joke and from this surprising first encounter grew a lasting friendship.

Some months later Steve Zuckerman, a student director, asked Sigourney to join the cast of *Darryl and Carol and Kenny and Jenny*, the first play written by Durang to be performed at Yale. It was a musical comedy which concerned the wild antics of a showbiz foursome. Sigourney was Jenny, a mentally unbalanced woman. Durang was mightily impressed by the way the actress handled the role; she played every freaky scene completely straight and the comedy seemed all the more eccentric and natural as a result. Watching from the wings, Durang sensed that Sigourney had a special rapport with the audience. At one point in the proceedings Sigourney sang a quaint little ditty called 'Better dead than sorry' while enduring shock treatment in a strait-jacket. Sigourney saw fit to make her own hat especially for the occasion. It had empty thread spools on each side, with wires protruding out of them. She played the scene in a frightening and brilliant way. Each time her singing was interrupted by the deadening 'buzz' of the shock treatment, Sigourney would momentarily freeze, her eyes would widen, and her head would fall slightly to one side, all in death-like silence. Then she would continue with the song. It was extremely effective. The show was a great success for all concerned and Sigourney's performance in the shock treatment scene must have lingered in the memories of the audience far beyond that closing night. Pitched together by this hastily rehearsed production Weaver and Durang soon emerged as committed friends. Before each performance they would dance backstage in an effort to limber up prior to their respective entrances. Some months later they were cast opposite one another in a children's show. Durang played an evil baron, while Sigourney was his miserable, troll-like wife who had a fondness for sado-masochism. Some children's show!

In addition to being close friends, they began to write wickedly satirical comedy material. Their most fruitful endeavour was a cabaret show, the idea for which stemmed from the singing classes they both attended, and the discovery that each of them liked the same kind of songs and enjoyed tampering with them, changing them around so they ended up sounding weird. This show later evolved into the Bertolt Brecht parody entitled *Das Lusitania Songspiel*, which was successfully presented off-Broadway some years later. Sigourney has admitted that the prevailing high seriousness at Yale would surely have destroyed her had it not been for the 'awful, insulting and trashy' cabaret material that she co-wrote with Durang. Sigourney's friendship and the activities she shared with the writer made her last few terms at Yale much more productive and less painful than those misspent early years. Durang and the others were responsible for the return of Sigourney's belief in herself as an actress and the restoration of her lost confidence. Without the encouragement and positive feedback of these people she might never have finished the course at Yale. She even began to win the belated approval of her teachers; alas, too late to heal the wounds. At last the faculty were starting to notice Sigourney, thanks to her performances in Durang's plays. They seemed to all agree that maybe the girl did show promise after all. But by and large she remained discouraged. With the notable exception of Durang's plays Sigourney was appalled by the inferior quality of most of the shows performed at the school. 'Some of them were just dreadful. Hated being in them, hated going to see them,' she told *Interview* magazine in July 1988. In her last year, Sigourney never even bothered to attend the plays she wasn't in, so great was her antipathy towards them.

Despite happy experiences with Durang and the rest of the playwrights, Sigourney was dangerously close to throwing in the towel. Acting was no longer the pleasure it had once been; the magical spark within her had been callously killed off by Yale's disciplined and over-intellectual approach to the theatre. To her the school had 'represented a narrowing of my horizons'. The lack of success and sheer drudgery had turned this once enthusiastic and idealistic youngster into an embittered and disillusioned 25-year-old. Before leaving Yale for good Sigourney visited a careers officer and asked for the unthinkable, 'a nice ordinary job', as a bank clerk.

3 *Unless You Know My Raincoat You'll Miss Me*

At the traditional and rather grandiose graduation ceremony which marks the departure of third year students from Yale the bruised and battered Sigourney still managed a wry smile and a final farewell prank that was pure Weaver. She arrived primly dressed in a blue blazer which she opened on stage, to reveal a large muslin target over her heart. The audience laughed, some even cheered. Whatever else Yale had managed to take away from Sigourney this delightful stunt proved that her sense of humour had survived intact.

With the benefit of hindsight one can see that perhaps Yale was the wrong kind of drama school for the wild and independently motivated Sigourney Weaver; the place was far too serious and political. Her father certainly thought so: he would have much preferred to see his daughter spending those three years studying across the road at the Yale Law School, then maybe she could have started her professional career as a lawyer on $20,000 a year. As it was, she just had the prospect of years shuffling from one lousy, no-hope audition to the next. This was a point of view that Sylvester had no hesitation in relaying to his daughter. But latterly, the wounds all but healed, the memory producing now only a dim and distant tinge of pain, Sigourney accepts the fact that Yale did instil in her skills and valuable lessons that were of some subsequent use. If she were to relive those times the actress would still feel inclined to attend a drama school, 'and I probably would end up going to Yale because I liked being with the playwrights'. By the time Sigourney arrived in New York, feeling alone and insignificant, just another struggling actress, she was already so accustomed to rejection that auditions weren't such a hardship. Sigourney had already had her fair share of adversity. The difficulty she had endured at Yale was now proving to be a great asset. Sometimes a little pain and suffering is good for the soul, it builds character and strengthens one's resilience. The school had taught her the art of perseverance, of how to cope under stressful and unpleasant circumstances. Many actors fresh from drama school find it tough coming to terms with the real world of acting. Sigourney herself was witness to the fall of numerous Yale contemporaries, many of whom had been the ones who were pampered and celebrated by the teachers; they had a much harder time adjusting than she did.

In contrast to the British actors who all swarm to London to begin their careers in the myriad of fringe theatres that litter the capital, American thespians have the option of two vastly different places – Los Angeles, where the sun and the movie industry are; or New York, where the more theatre-conscious actors tend to prosper. For Sigourney the choice had been a simple one; after all, she was first and foremost a stage actress, although she was later to attain fame in the cinema. A return to New York was also a nostalgic trip back to the memories of her childhood. Unfortunately, one of the more painful aspects of her youth had reappeared to haunt her in the present. Once again Sigourney's great height was causing her grievous personal disappointment. On one occasion a producer was unwilling to use her because she was taller than the leading man.

'Look,' she said. 'Why don't I paint a pair of shoes on my feet and I'll play the role barefoot.'

The producer thought deeply about the idea. 'I don't think that would work, Sigourney,' he finally answered.

She was amazed by his response, she hadn't meant her suggestion to be taken seriously. It was a joke. 'And the idiot had taken me seriously.'

Sigourney's first year out of Yale was extremely tough. The big agents complained about her height and kept trying to typecast her as a high society girlfriend, the kind of superficial female who nods politely at cocktail functions, pours the drinks, and stands in a state of servility behind her centre-stage boyfriend, the kind of sickeningly outdated character that Sigourney would rather lose a major part of her anatomy than play. Despite these initial setbacks, fused with the feeling of disillusionment that still preoccupied her after the trials and tribulations of Yale, Sigourney fought back with a vengeance. At auditions she was never afraid to be daring. 'I would just use the five minutes I had to play the hell out of the part.' This seemingly reckless approach was due to the fact that Sigourney felt she had nothing much to lose; on the whole she didn't really care if she got the part or not. Unlike the majority of her fellow Yale hopefuls, hell-bent on acting glory, Sigourney was a ferment of mixed emotions, still undecided about whether she really wanted to pursue a career in the theatre or not. At the time the idea of quitting, untypical though it might seem, was a real possibility. After Yale it was Sigourney's intention never to be part of show business again. But she, more than anyone else, knew the truth about the hazards and pitfalls of the profession, thanks to her entertainment-soaked background. This had left her uniquely equipped to cope with the harsh realities that actors must often face. Many of her Yale colleagues had perhaps grown up under the illusion that the world of acting was some kind of fairy-tale land full of opportunity, whereas the young Sigourney had seen with her own eyes how cruel and unpredictable it could be. Being an actor can be one of the most satisfying jobs there is, a great way to earn a living, but the chances of reaching stardom and the big money league are very slim indeed. If one can just enjoy the work and have a good time with one's fellow artists, Sigourney believes, that's reason enough to be in the business. The fact that she now commands millions of dollars per film is merely a by-product of the career she loves.

In New York Sigourney's greatest fear was that she would be unable to support herself financially if she decided to go ahead with her acting career. The idea of working in a bank seemed for a while to be her best short-term prospect. She thought that as a bank teller she would be surrounded by money all day and even though the cash wasn't hers the handling of those fresh bills and crisp notes would make her feel more secure. 'It sounded like a lovely job.' But she resisted the temptation of a nice, steady job and instead opted for the erratic and perilous life of an actor, safe in the knowledge that she was in a far more fortuitous position than many of the other actors in New York who operated without a safety-net and could easily end up on the scrap heap after years of hard graft if they failed. Sigourney was lucky in that her family were rich and could bail her out if she ever hit rock-bottom. During Sigourney's first six months in New York, until she settled in and found work, Sylvester supported her. But after that she was on her own. Her first theatre job was quite exceptional, an understudy role in *The Constant Wife*, with Ingrid Bergman, a touring play that was all set for a Broadway run. Sigourney had been an admirer of Bergman for a number of years and here was a marvellous opportunity, early on in her career, to watch a true professional at work. The veteran actress proved to be a great role model for the young Sigourney. The play was directed by Sir John Gielgud, another legend of the theatre. This was Sigourney's first professional job in the legitimate theatre world and one which served as a source of great encouragement to her. It gave her a renewed confidence in both herself and her talents, and also the strength to succeed. 'Suddenly I thought maybe you're not wrong to have chosen the theatre,' Sigourney said to *The Sunday Telegraph Magazine*, in June 1983. 'If Sir John wants to have you in his company you can't be as bad as they say.' But this lucky first break failed to lead to more equally distinguished theatrical employment. The great New York directors were hardly falling over themselves to hire her. So it was back to the treadmill and the soul-destroying daily routine of auditioning.

Meanwhile her Yale comrade, Christopher Durang, was looking for actors to appear in one of his new plays. He immediately remembered the effervescent and talented Weaver and gave her a call. This offer of work, which may have saved Sigourney from any thoughts she still harboured about a job in civvy street away from the bright lights and the grease paint, lead to the actress's first professional on-stage role in the off-Broadway production of Durang's play *The Nature and the Purpose of the Universe*. Once again Durang had arrived on the scene at a turning point in Sigourney's life. *Universe* was followed by another Durang fringe production, *Titanic*, in which Sigourney played a young woman with a multiple personality and a penchant for violence. True to form, this Durang offering was another weird and wonderful journey into black surrealism. The part of Lidia, the daughter of the Titanic's captain, was an incredibly complex and demanding role to come to grips with because of the strange nature of the character. At one point in the play Lidia reveals to the audience that she once kept a hedgehog in her vagina. (How's that for surreal?) Just when one is getting used to her crackpot nature, Lidia becomes Harriet, an embittered lesbian. By the finale she has assumed yet another identity and, dressed in a black evening-gown and brandishing a pistol, she kills her own parents in cold blood, then sits and waits and prays for the great ship to sink. The play was only moderately successful, but Sigourney made quite an impact as Lidia. Durang thought she was fabulous in the role.

Sigourney spent the next few years auditioning endlessly. Like her father, Sigourney's boundless energy was self-evident as she travelled from theatre to theatre searching for jobs. For most actors the sheer toil of looking for work can be both a demoralizing and wretched experience. In Sigourney's case things were significantly different. She had been so fundamentally rejected prior to her New York experience that she found the city a playground of opportunities. Each day she could look for openings in the variety of trade papers available and then go and audition. There were no teachers around to stop her this time. 'To me New York was the promised land.' Sigourney's new-found confidence and belief in her abilities prevented her from cracking under the pressures inherent in the auditioning process. She managed to take all of them, even the really important ones, in her stride. For her, the thrill was in constantly entering new theatres, standing alone on a dark, cold stage performing to a wide range of directors who mostly sat in indifference among the shadows of the stalls. Often on these occasions Sigourney would use her own inner fear as a kind of energy. This is stage fright and a great many actors use this to psyche themselves up before leaving the wings to face a packed house. One of Sigourney's old drama teachers used to say, 'If you're not nervous before a show, worry!' 'That's adrenalin. I sometimes miss those days where I could walk in off the street and audition for something, and no one knew who I was.'

Annoyingly, when she did get a stage part it was usually a silly comedy role or a difficult, joyless character. Because of her height she never seemed to get the chance to play romantic leads or the heroine. Sometimes there was no work at all. Those dark spells of unemployment were rough. Sigourney would sit alone in her little flat in reflective mood, mulling over in her mind whether or not she had made the right decision.

Eventually, Sigourney reached the point, with a steady flow of money and jobs coming in, when she knew she could support herself. She could now relax a bit; her financial pressures had been lessened considerably. The actress had come a long way from the days when a good week meant that she had been able to audition for a television commercial. Now she was managing to find work in a number of plays with off-Broadway and road company groups. She won particular acclaim as Judith in Albert Innaurato's *Gemini*, before Kathleen Turner took over the role for its Broadway run. She was also fortunate enough to win regular work in showcases (events where actors perform scenes from plays etc. to a specially invited audience of agents and producers), where jobs were almost impossible to come by. The memory of auditions haunted her for years afterwards. Everytime she visited the Public Theatre and saw signs up on the notice-board announcing that general auditions were being held upstairs, she would feel a knot in the pit of her stomach as she recalled the weeks of hard work that had gone into preparing for hers, and the hope that the casting people would still be conscious after seeing twenty or more other actors that same day. Sigourney also found time to study drama with Nikos Psacharo-Poulos and Robert Lewis, and dance with Carmen de Lavallade, as well as regularly attending a New York actor's workshop, a course which taught her more about her craft than all those wasted years at Yale put together. Even after Sigourney's big break in *Alien* she still managed to attend the workshop twice weekly whenever she was in town. Stardom never went to her head; she still felt that the lessons were worthwhile and beneficial.

1977 was a good year for Sigourney. She broke into television and the movies and also managed to win her most coveted theatre job to date, a small role in John Guare's

Marco Polo Sings a Solo directed by Mel Shapiro and produced by Joseph Papp at the Public Theatre. At last her career seemed to be really taking off. Guare's play, like many of Durang's efforts, was a touch bizarre. Sigourney played a Swedish maid whose job it was to clean the glacier on which most of the action took place. Later in the proceedings Sigourney's stomach lit up when she was artificially impregnated by an astronaut. Despite the show's comical pretensions Sigourney gained much recognition, mainly due to the auspicious company in which she found herself – Joel Grey, who won an Oscar as the MC in *Cabaret*; Madeline Kahn, a most gifted comedienne noted for her performances in a string of Mel Brooks movies; and Anne Jackson, who one day realized the extent of the play's strangeness when she overheard Sigourney ask the director, 'Should I clean off the sky, too?' Not only were these actors the most experienced Sigourney had yet worked with, but *Marco Polo* also gave her the opportunity to work with one of New York's most celebrated theatre people, Joseph Papp. Sigourney later appeared in *New Jerusalem*, another Papp production at the Public Theatre.

After years of acting in arty and experimental off-Broadway plays, Sigourney suddenly found herself in the conservative world of commercial television. The transition from the stage to TV wasn't easy, but she soon began to receive offers of work, primarily for supporting or brief guest spot roles. In common with the majority of American actors Sigourney ended up working in one or other of the never-ending legion of daily soap operas that plague US television. She appeared in the fondly forgotten *Somerset*, alongside the young Ted Danson, playing a woman whose ambition was to become America's first female president. She also appeared as Laura Wheeler in *The Best of Families*, a grand eight-part drama set in the United States during the late nineteenth century, which premièred in October 1977. The story centred around the activities of three families from contrasting social backgrounds, and the series was ambitious and expertly crafted. The cast featured a then unknown actor who was to cross Sigourney Weaver's professional path on more than one occasion: William Hurt. The series, however, fared badly with critics and public alike. Slightly better for Sigourney was a sizeable role in the television dramatization of John Cheevers' short story *The Sorrows of Gin*.

1977 was also the year of Sigourney Weaver's feature film début. In complete contrast to the multitude of actors who have gone on to claim stardom but whose early movies were turkeys or long forgotten relics, Sigourney made her début in an acknowledged masterpiece of modern cinema, Woody Allen's *Annie Hall*. Her audition was the archetypal actor's nightmare. Sigourney was nervous enough (she was a great admirer of the comedian's work), but when her performance was greeted by Allen's customary silence, panic took over. In a state of dismay, she struggled to find her way out and stumbled into a broom cupboard by mistake. She eventually found the exit door and left in a sullen and highly embarrassed state. But she got the part, much to her surprise, although she later had to forsake it due to prior stage commitments. Luckily, Allen was still keen to use her, so he arranged for Sigourney to appear in a walk-on role close to the end of the film. She played Alvy's date outside a theatre. So small was her contribution that Sigourney later joked, 'Unless you know my raincoat you'll miss me.' *Annie Hall* went on to pick up four well-deserved Oscars, including those for Best Picture and Best Direction. One wonders just why Weaver and Allen have never collaborated on another film together, with Sigourney in a more prominent role. They were born to be professionally intertwined. Each in their own way is a quintessential New Yorker. They were both born there and lived and worked in the city in later life. Sigourney would have been perfect in the Meryl Streep role in *Manhattan* or as Barbara Hershey's character in *Hannah and Her Sisters*.

As 1977 moved into 1978 Sigourney Weaver, now approaching thirty, had still to find that elusive first big break, that initial springboard which every actor needs in order to launch his or her career. Unperturbed, she continued to send out her *bio* and portfolio to every casting agent in town and to audition for stage roles or supporting parts in films. At one such audition she failed to persuade director Mark Rydell to cast her as a lesbian in the Bette Midler *tour de force*, *The Rose*. So it was back to being battered by the constant, inglorious round of auditions, of raised hopes and subsequent disappointments. Despite her earlier fortitude the constant slog of prostituting herself for little reward was now taking its toll. Matters finally came to a head when she lost a cherished leading role in an experimental piece called *History of the American Film*. Her failure to secure the part was made that much more miserable since it had been written by Christopher Durang expressly with her in mind. During this tense point in Weaver's life another old ex-Yale classmate, Kate Macgregor-Stewart came to her rescue. She suggested to Sigourney that she enrol in one of the courses at EST, a psychological training programme, where she would be able to develop a healthy philosophy that would allow her to contest the arbitrariness of the industry. Kate was quite persistent about Sigourney joining and every time the two met Kate would bring up the subject of EST.

'I want you to take the training,' she would say.

'Why?' Weaver would invariably ask.

'Because I love you,' was the simple answer.

Finally Sigourney signed up. The course wasn't a revelation, but nor was it the humiliating experience that the various newspaper articles on EST that she had cursorily read had led her to believe. In fact, she enjoyed the experience immensely. She would sit in a large room amongst three hundred people, all of whom would talk very personally about themselves, dredging up all sorts of problems and hang-ups from the innermost sanctums of their souls and putting them on public exhibition. It was a form of mass exorcism. For an actor, the atmosphere at such meetings was quite stimulating and most gratifying. 'I was amazed by all the human stories intermingling.' These sessions proved to be the foundation on which a previously shy Sigourney Weaver was able to build her confidence and really communicate with the outside world and the people in it. 'I was taught as a child never to talk about myself, never to talk about my emotions,' she revealed to *Interview* magazine in July 1988. 'Of course, now I talk about myself constantly. Now I have to take reverse EST.' Again Sigourney's parents felt uneasy about their daughter's latest activity. To try and put their minds to rest Sigourney invited them to a guest seminar. It was a disaster. Elizabeth never took off her coat and flatly refused to have a name tag put on. She came out complaining that everyone smelled. Sigourney was convinced that her parents thought she had now turned into a 'Jesus freak'.

'A very valuable place' is how Sigourney describes EST. The course helped her to regain control over her career enormously. Friends began to notice in her a new sense of independence and purpose; she seemed to be in a much more healthy and happier frame of mind. Soon she was heavily committed to EST and became involved in one programme called The Hunger Project, an honourable, if slightly naïve, effort to feed the starving of the world. In the middle of such a weighty endeavour the offer of a leading role in a movie appeared irrelevant. But the movie happened to be *Alien*, and the part of Ripley was to change her life overnight.

4 *In Space No One Can Hear You Scream*

Blessed with a new and mighty inner strength thanks to the teachings of EST, Sigourney's professional life couldn't have been more different. Her career was in the dumps. She had just opened in the off-Broadway play, *The Conquering Event*, and was gallantly trying to be objective about the opening night's foul reviews, when she received a phone call from Mary Goldberg, an independent agent who was a keen admirer of her work. Goldberg arranged for Sigourney to meet Walter Hill, David Giler and Gordon Carroll, a group of creative producers who had come to New York looking for someone to play Ripley, the female protagonist in a new and ambitious science fiction film called *Alien*. They had brought with them a list of actresses that they were all keen to interview. Sigourney had been highly recommended to them and was in the first batch they wanted to see. Although she had no film experience to speak of she had done enough good stage work to warrant consideration.

The role of Ripley was an arduous one. She was a tough, unglamorous and uncompromising character and the person to portray her needed to be equally tough and independent. Also, as the sole survivor of a space expedition, Sigourney, if chosen for the part, would occupy more screen minutes than her experienced co-stars. Amazingly, she seemed to display blatant indifference to what was a golden opportunity, the chance of the lead role in a major Hollywood movie, a once in a lifetime offer that other actors might have killed for. But there were more weighty matters occupying Sigourney's mind, namely her loyalty and commitment to The Hunger Project, and her concerns about ending the plight of the world's starving millions. Nevertheless, the interview went ahead and was a great success. Despite her detached attitude to the whole proceedings, Sigourney still managed to excite the curiosity of her would-be employers. The men asked if she would read the script overnight and return for further discussions the following morning. In near-disregard for the obvious advantages of being involved in *Alien*, Sigourney harboured grave reservations about the project. 'I didn't want to play this awful part in this awful movie', she recalled to *You* magazine in November 1989. She had not suffered the indignities of Yale just to star in a low-grade horror flick. 'I mean, to do science fiction was below even me. I didn't know *Alien* was this masterpiece. I thought it was this big blob of yellow jelly running around.'

The actress was most critical of the screenplay after the initial read-through. She found the story very bleak and unappealing, and felt that the characters failed to relate to one another and were too impersonal and bloodless. When Sigourney returned the following day she made her opinions known in blunt fashion to the producers, much to the open consternation of a casting agent who was heard to mutter, 'Stupid woman! Don't you realize this is your big break?' This was indeed near-suicidal behaviour for an unknown on the threshold of her first starring role. But Sigourney had always been encouraged to speak her mind while working on new plays with new playwrights. Being brought up in the business, existing around entertainers, producers and the like from childhood, also helped enormously to produce a supremely confident actress, never afraid, even at the very beginning of her career, to speak out, to make public any professional misgivings. 'I don't know if people in movies are used to that. I would think they should be.' By speaking out she can best gauge how receptive her fellow workers are. She knew that if Hill and the other producers were at all serious about hiring her then they would accept her criticisms and encourage her views on the character of Ripley and the script. The film's director Ridley Scott was present at that second meeting. After talking with him at some length and studying the designs for the film and for the eponymous monster, Sigourney began to realize that *Alien* was going to be a very innovative picture. Suddenly, the project was starting to engage her interest.

Everyone agreed that Sigourney was perfect for Ripley. After months of searching, the right actress had at last been found. But the final decision as to whether she was worth the time and expense of a screen test lay with Alan Ladd jnr. (who had never even heard of her), head of 20th Century Fox, the legendary studio, which had agreed to back the costly production. From the outset, Fox had had mixed feelings about an unknown taking on the mantle of such a big, important role. They would have preferred to have seen Faye Dunaway or Jane Fonda fill Ripley's shoes. Just weeks after those first tentative meetings in New York, Sigourney was on her way to meet Ladd in Los Angeles. Attired in casual garb (a pair of tatty jeans, a T-shirt, and hooker boots), because the airline had managed to lose her luggage, Sigourney Weaver came face to face with some of filmdom's most important executives. Surprisingly, Sigourney was totally unfazed by the situation, 'Because I was so busy thinking about ending world hunger,' she told *Interview* magazine in July 1988. 'If I hadn't been in an unambitious place philosophically, I think I would have tried harder.' In the end Ladd decided that a screen test was indeed a worthwhile proposition and wanted her in London within forty-eight hours. Shepperton Studios was the destination and awaiting her was a gruelling day of testing on a little set that Ridley had built for the actress. Suffering from jet lag, and a stranger in a strange land, Sigourney managed to handle the immense pressure that had suddenly been thrust upon her with admirable courage and professionalism. She and the English crew worked almost non-stop throughout the afternoon and into the early hours of the following morning. By the end Sigourney was utterly exhausted and almost drained of energy. Considering the role of Ripley was to launch her career, it is amazing to learn that only the day before this important screen test did the actress finally decide that she wanted to play the character. One wonders where Sigourney would be today if she had declined the offer.

Flying back home to New York the next day, Sigourney mentally prepared herself for the weeks, perhaps months, that she would have to wait before she heard if the part was hers or not. Sigourney had not been long back at her apartment, and was listening to Lena Horne singing 'I've Got the World on a String' when the phone rang. On the other end of the line she expected to hear the voice of one of her acting colleagues asking how the interview went, or a casting agent with news of a local audition. Instead, to her surprise, she found herself talking to one of the *Alien* producers. Sigourney listened dumbfounded as he congratulated her on winning the part. She was overjoyed; she could hardly contain her excitement. Soon Sigourney's entire circle of friends had heard the news that she had won the star part in a major movie. Sigourney's mother, however, was curiously restrained when she heard the happy tidings. In the script there was a semi-romantic scene in which the no-nonsense Ripley walks into the captain's cabin, unzips her suit and announces, 'I need some relief.' Elizabeth, on reading this section of the screenplay, turned to Sigourney, took off her glasses and said, 'Nude?' The thought of her own precious daughter appearing stark naked on the cinema screen in front of countless millions, shocked Elizabeth deeply. Such a thing had never happened in her day. Despite this being one of Scott's favourite moments in *Alien* (they had built a special chair for the couple to make love on), the scene was scrapped, much to the relief of Sigourney who had thought it 'a ludicrous idea'. How could anyone cavort naked in a room when a murderous alien monster was running amok outside?

In other, much less progressive science fiction, the character of Ripley would most certainly have been your average macho male, all brawn and bullets 'a sort of Burt Reynolds in outer space', in Sigourney's words. Originally, all seven crew members of the spaceship *Nostromo* were male. Eternal sex symbol Paul Newman was the makers' first choice to play Ripley. It was Alan Ladd jnr. who ordered that the roles of Ripley and Lambert be played by women. This was a wise move on his part and gave *Alien* a unique quality that its rivals lacked: a woman had become the hero in a genre where men usually reigned supreme. The most significant factor was that the screenwriters did not alter one word of Ripley's dialogue when they changed her sex. Certainly on-screen there is nothing 'feminine' about her character. She is seen as a self-reliant working woman dealing with responsibilities. This was a factor that heavily influenced Sigourney's decision to play Ripley. Here at last was a great film role for a woman who wouldn't have to fall in love with the leading man or be a damsel in distress. Ripley was strong and resourceful and could carry out her duties just as well as any man. Although the film's subject matter scarcely appealed to women, when *Alien* opened in America some feminist groups hailed the work as a minor but valid breakthrough in the fight towards an acceptance and awareness of women's growing equality in the modern age.

The only obvious concession to Ripley's sexuality comes near to the end of the picture when she strips down to a T-shirt and a pair of tight briefs. Ridley Scott decided to include this sequence in order to feminize Ripley slightly and to stress her vulnerability, after some observers had claimed that she was too hard and unsympathetic. The actress was quick to quieten allegations that the semi-nude scene was executed purely for thrills, a piece of female exploitation. Sigourney was upset when people accused her of demeaning herself by blindly performing a crude space strip-tease. She believed that Ripley's actions in the scene are totally justified. She is tired and dirty and wants to get rid of her sweaty, bloodstained clothes by taking a shower before entering hypersleep. For Ripley this is a perfectly natural thing to do. (Originally Ridley Scott wanted much more nudity in the film, of the matter-of-fact variety, crew members walking about naked and the like, which Sigourney approved of. Their bare flesh would contrast nicely with the harsh surroundings of the spacecraft in which they worked.) She was so responsive to the idea of the nude scene that she was even prepared to strip entirely (a move blocked by Fox, who feared that the sight of Sigourney's naked body would jeopardize the film's chances of box office success in Catholic countries). Sigourney called the decision 'a cop out'. Perhaps this was just as well. Even partially naked, Sigourney provoked an inordinate amount of fan mail, some of which was very strange indeed. She also courted some bizarre attention; men began to follow her around. Thankfully, by the early eighties such mad worship had eased off, but Sigourney was left mentally scarred. 'It made me pull right back from the movies.'

The plot of *Alien* has much in common with the formulaic fifties monster movie, but is updated with hi-tech production values and graphic violence. The crew of the starship *Nostromo* are awoken from hypersleep when their on-board computer intercepts what appears to be an SOS signal emanating from a mysterious planet. On this desolate new world the crew discover a derelict craft of unknown origin. One of the party, Kane (John Hurt), finds an ante-chamber filled with eggs containing live organisms, one of which violently attaches itself to his face. Kane is carried back to the *Nostromo* in a coma, but the alien creature gestating within his frail body is soon released into the ship and embarks upon a reign of terror. The idea for *Alien* sprang from the fertile imaginations of Dan O'Bannon (one of the creative team behind the cult science fiction classic *Dark Star*), and Ronald Shusett. The concept of an invincible monster running rampant aboard a space vessel was what initially so fascinated O'Bannon. At the time, the two writers were broke and O'Bannon was sleeping on his colleague's sofa. The script, which was then called *Star Beast*, was completed in three months, and was intended to be a low-budget movie costing no more than a half-million dollars. The project passed from studio to studio and was rejected repeatedly. Then, in 1977, Brandywine Productions, who thought the idea had all the makings of a hit, optioned the script. Substantial work on the screenplay was essential if its potential was to be realized. Walter Hill, a partner in Brandywine with Gordon Carroll and David Giler, and a pedigree director in his own right (*The Warriors, 48 HRS*, and *Red Heat*), handled the first rewrite. The final shooting script was by Hill and Giler, although they received no screen credit. Whilst retaining the basic plot and structure, the two writers were to add significant new material to the work. It was during the rewrites, for example, that the sex of Ripley was changed and an interesting subplot was introduced that made Ash (Ian Holm), one of the crew, an android with orders to return the alien to earth for scientific/military purposes. The owners of the *Nostromo* know all along that the SOS beacon is in reality a warning signal. They have deliberately sent the crew into danger in order to procure the extraterrestrial. Ripley and the rest are all expendable. This cynical view of the ethics of a corporation prepared to put profits before the lives of its workers gives *Alien* a nice cutting edge. Hill and Giler also discarded some of O'Bannon's more bizarre ideas, most notably one scene in which the alien eggs are found in a giant pyramid belonging to an ancient civilization.

The new, revised script caught the attention of 20th Century Fox. But no one, not even Walter Hill himself, wanted to direct the movie. Then Sandy Liberson, head of European production at Fox, sent the screenplay to Ridley Scott, a young British director with only one feature film to his credit. Scott read the script in about forty minutes and was enthralled by its simplicity and impact. He immediately agreed to become involved. A graduate of London's Royal Academy of Art, Scott worked for a number of years at the BBC where he entered a training programme which led to directorial chores on shows like *Z Cars*. The lucrative world of advertising soon beckoned and Scott spent a decade honing his craft on commercials, including those famous sepia-tint Hovis ads, in the process of establishing his own successful company. Many of Scott's technical associates from those days worked with him on *Alien*, and his background in design and art contributed greatly to the innovative visual style he instilled into the film. Scott's début cinema work in 1977 was the well-crafted *The Duellists*, which won a special jury prize at the Cannes Film Festival. But it was the success of *Alien* that secured Scott's future as a major film-making talent. His post-*Alien* films have included *Blade Runner* and *Black Rain*.

The director's primary concern during pre-production was what the creature of the title was going to look like on screen. With very few exceptions movie monsters tend to look like actors dressed up in a rubber suit, they are rarely convincing. After rejecting various sketches of blobs and dinosaurs, beasts with two heads, bulging eyes – the lot – and close to giving up altogether, O'Bannon showed the director a book of paintings by the Swiss surrealist H.R. Giger. One drawing of a demon-like creature instantly captivated Scott. 'It was the most frightening thing I'd ever seen.' Giger was hired to create the alien, the derelict spacecraft and the eerie surface of the strange planetoid. Giger's art is a combination of the sexually macabre and the sickeningly bizarre. His paintings are full of nightmarish images and phallic symbolism;

striking juxtapositions of bone, flesh and machinery which are cold, yet hauntingly beautiful. 'Mortuary eroticism' one astute critic called his work. Giger's otherworldly designs were influential in steering *Alien* away from the look of conventional science fiction cinema and are a highlight of the film, especially the interior of the spacecraft with its vagina-like passages and intricate bone-like designs. Sigourney remembers giving her parents a guided tour around the large and forbidding set. Both Sylvester and Elizabeth were quite shocked by the spectacle. 'Very interesting,' they said, gulping. 'Very interesting.'

In Giger's paintings humanoid shapes like bones and spines often take on the appearance of machine parts. This concept is used to great dramatic effect in *Alien* where machines appear to be organic, while live organisms seem to have a mechanistic quality. The artist imagined the monster to be half-human, half-machine. The materials used in the construction of the alien included polyester, rubber, animal meat, bones and oysters. Once Giger's alien had been conceived, the problem remained of how to bring it to life. Scott dreaded the idea of using a man in a monster-suit. At one stage the makers were all set to use stop-motion animation (à la Ray Harryhausen) to move the creature. Although an actor in a costume was used for some shots, ninety per cent of the alien footage in the finished film were close-ups of a mechanical head created by Carlo Rambaldi, the man who later breathed life into ET. To keep alive a feeling of terror and apprehension in the audience, Scott cleverly made sure that the alien was seen only sporadically, in short, sharp bursts. The full view of the creature was saved for the film's final gripping minutes.

With a budget of $8 million, *Alien* began filming at Shepperton on 3 July 1978. The decision to make the picture at an English studio was a logical one. Ever since *Star Wars* in 1977 many of the big-budget American effects movies had come to Britain. It was cheaper to film in the UK and the studios boasted some of the best technicians in the world. *Superman, Indiana Jones, Batman*, and the *Star Wars* trilogy have all been made in England with British expertise, but without alas, local money. When Sigourney Weaver flew into London, prepared and ready for the long and rigorous work that lay ahead, she arrived in the middle of a bitter row that was taking place between 20th Century Fox and the British actors union, Equity. *Alien*'s producers had asked for four work permits for the American actors, Tom Skerritt, Yaphet Kotto, Harry Dean Stanton and Sigourney Weaver herself. Equity approved the first two but recommended to the Department of Employment that Weaver's and Stanton's be revoked. Because the film was being made in England the union felt that the roles should have gone to British actors. Sigourney's rise to superstardom was almost halted before it had a chance to begin. The producers gallantly argued the case that no one but Sigourney Weaver could play Ripley and just days before shooting was due to begin the Department of Employment overruled Equity's objections. During filming Sigourney felt there was some resentment towards her because she came from New York and had landed the best part. She sometimes found the hostile atmosphere at Shepperton a little difficult to cope with. The segregation between leading and supporting players in films is something that Sigourney has always found stupid and distasteful. But she didn't take the abuse lightly and hit back in fighting style by way of the British tabloid press. 'Hardly any American actors get to play in London,' she told the *Daily Express* in September 1979. 'But Broadway is populated by Britons picking up all our prizes. There should be a fairer rate of exchange.'

A complete newcomer to the world of film, Sigourney was a little unsure about what was expected of her. So inexperienced was she that for the first week Scott had to tell the actress not to look *into* the camera. Her initiation was made easier by the assistance she received from her co-stars; they all helped her to settle into the day-to-day process of movie making and taught her basic film technique, such as how to hit her mark (which means standing in the right position in front of the camera). She was also able to learn a great deal from working with actors from various dramatic backgrounds. With the English members of the cast, like Ian Holm, the scenes were played word-perfect; whereas, when she acted with the Americans, notably Yaphet Kotto, a lot of improvising took place. 'However an actor worked, I was willing to work with him that way.' Indeed she would have liked to have seen more on-set improvisation. She feels that this would have brought the cast closer together and made them into the ensemble they should have been. Ridley Scott was most helpful and the two of them got on very well. Each day he would invite Sigourney behind the camera. In this way she was able to see that *Alien* 'was an incredible film to be part of'. Weaver particularly admired Scott's directorial flair and visual sense (although she was less impressed by the way he dealt with actors), and respected the man's brutal honesty. If there was something wrong on the set or in an actor's performance he would make his feelings known straightaway. There was no time for diplomacy when Ridley Scott was around. 'In an industry where there's so much bullshit, I really appreciated his just getting to the point.' Sigourney also found that Scott's vision of Ripley and his ideas for presenting the character on screen were identical to her own. At the London audition Sigourney was made to wear a series of unsuitable costumes which made her feel like 'Jackie Onassis in space', until Ridley began to search through a mountain of clothes and pulled out an old grey astronaut's practice uniform which he threw over to Sigourney to try on. It was perfect, 'and that's the one I ended up wearing'. Scott and Sigourney seemed to be on the same creative wavelength.

In an effort to familiarize herself with the character before filming, Sigourney researched into the kinds of women who sign up to become astronauts and work on American space missions. She was surprised to learn that, despite their extraordinary achievements and limitless courage, many of them were plain, ordinary people. She therefore decided to play Ripley as a very down-to-earth woman, not exceptional, just performing her job to the best of her abilities. Only at the end, alone and face to face with the monster, does Ripley become a hero, finding out that she has hidden strengths and valour. In spite of Sigourney's obvious fondness for Ripley she later confessed that the character was probably the most unoriginal and one dimensional she had ever been asked to play. Sigourney originally wanted to play Lambert (Veronica Cartwright), a high-spirited individual, always in a jovial mood and telling jokes while everyone else around her is becoming hysterical. Only later does she finally crack up. Sigourney clearly identified with Lambert. This is how

Sigourney believes that she herself would act in a similar situation. However, when Cartwright was cast in the role, she and Scott drastically altered the character.

To portray the weary crew of the space-tug *Nostromo*, Scott deliberately chose a cast of character actors rather than star names. The compelling assortment of players give stark and realistic performances, even if the film's naturalism is occasionally overplayed. The sound is sometimes inaudible and the characters speak in monotonous tones, often simultaneously. Nevertheless, it is interesting to watch the acting styles of Sigourney Weaver, Tom Skerritt *et al.* mesh with the classically trained English actors. One of Scott's intentions was to convey the sheer mundanity and tedium of a long space trip. To this end, the crew are a scruffy, bored and unattractive bunch who travel across the galaxy, not in any *Star Trek*-inspired idealistic quest to discover new life forms and planets, but to rape the solar system of its precious oils and minerals, bring them back to earth and then share in the profits. Their living quarters are cramped and littered with throw-away domestic items, their ship is an ugly, brooding, utilitarian machine. *Alien* is very much a realistic film whose strength lies in character and plot development rather than in glossy special effects. However, early on in the production two factions emerged, each with different views about what direction the picture should take. One insisted on more science fiction influence, while the other wanted to minimalize the fantasy element. Scott himself saw *Alien* as a 'vicious shocker', an unrelenting journey into the very heart of terror, a film about fear of the unknown, much more of a thriller than a standard horror/sci-fi vehicle. This was a conscious effort to move his work away from the futuristic chic that plagued the genre, exemplified by the brightly lit and antiseptic modernism of *2001*. His future-world is dirty and grimy. Giger's sets are darkly gothic in atmosphere and the rooms and passageways of the *Nostromo* are bleak and claustrophobic places. These dimly lit corridors are designed to give the impression that the alien, which, with its near-metallic appearance can become camouflaged amongst the pipes and ducts of the ship, is about to leap out at the audience at any moment. *Alien* has none of the glamour or romanticism of, say, *Star Wars*. '*Alien* is to *Star Wars* what the Rolling Stones are to The Beatles' said producer David Giler to *Cinefantastique* in 1979. 'It's a nasty *Star Wars*.' Scott's view of the future clashes violently with the hopeful, optimistic vision of George Lucas and Stephen Spielberg. The space creatures of *Close Encounters of the Third Kind* and *ET* are friendly, even lovable. Scott is decidedly more pessimistic about other life forms.

During the sixteen weeks of principal photography, film chiefs were so worried that pictures or details about *Alien* would leak out to an increasingly curious press that they ordered full-scale security around the studio. On one of the entrance doors to the soundstages a large notice printed in bold red and black lettering warned 'Absolutely no visitors without written permission from the production manager'.

The most famous and talked about scene in *Alien* is the one in which the creature, in graphic fashion, bursts out of John Hurt's chest. Scott wanted this sequence to be as bloody and as gruesome as possible, so he arranged for fresh offal to be collected from a nearby abattoir. Hurt was not in the least bit perturbed by the gory process that was unfolding before him, and drank white wine and casually smoked as members of the effects crew loaded his false chest with bits of liver and entrails. The rest of the cast were kept in the dark about what was going to happen. Scott wished to capture live on camera their immediate response to the bloody spectacle. When the false chest was detonated and the infant alien emerged from the mangled remains of Hurt's stomach, the actors recoiled in genuine fright. Veronica Cartwright, in particular, got drenched in blood and was in a state of shock for hours afterwards. Derek Vanlint, the director of photography, was actually physically ill when he first watched this scene and had to walk out of the rushes screening. Scott employed comparable techniques in those moments which involved the actors with the full-scale alien. 'We didn't rehearse very much at all because the effects were so good that Ridley wanted to capture our instantaneous reactions to them,' Sigourney told *What's on in London* in September 1979. One effect that nearly went disastrously wrong involved the heavy-duty flame-throwers that some members of the cast had to operate. During filming Sigourney had a near miss with one of these lethal devices. One of the deadly flames missed her by just three inches.

In the working version of *Alien*, which ran for well over two hours, far more of the monster was seen. One nasty sequence that ultimately ended up on the cutting room floor involved Ripley, who on hearing human weeping discovers Captain Dallas and Brett in the alien's lair. Both men have been impregnated by the beast and are in the process of turning into cocoon-like forms. Dallas begs Ripley to kill them. She answers his pleas with a quick burst from her flame-thrower. Unfortunately, by omitting this significant sequence the audience is made to think that the alien is just wantonly eating the crew one by one, whereas in reality the creature is only carrying out what it has been biologically programmed to do: to preserve and continue its own species. Sigourney was bitterly disappointed that this scene, which contained her most dramatic moment of the entire film, was dropped. 'For those selfish acting reasons I wanted to see it.'

20th Century Fox held high hopes for *Alien* and released the film in the USA on 25 May 1979, the second anniversary of the release of Fox's most prestigious money-maker *Star Wars*. The studio were quietly confident that *Alien* would be just as big a summer hit. The pre-release publicity for *Alien* was massive, spawning the now legendary ad line 'In space no one can hear you scream'. The campaign worked and box-office records were broken across the country. Some cinemas ran the film twenty-four hours a day non-stop in order to cope with the demand. Journalists, who had been specifically asked not to divulge too much of the film's plot to their readers, could not help but get caught up in *Alien* fever which was beginning to spread throughout the States. Headlines about the movie gripping the nation in a 'stranglehold of extraterrestrial terror' were not uncommon. Many hailed Scott's work as one of the greatest shockers of all time. In just a matter of weeks *Alien* had become a cinematic sensation. It was described as 'Hollywood's most efficient moneymaking machine of the summer' by *Time* magazine. The picture eventually amassed a US box-office gross of $40 million. In Britain, *Alien* opened amidst great hype on 6 September and was the fourth highest earner of the year. Later in the month Sigourney flew to Spain to attend the showing of *Alien* at the San Sebastian film festival. Despite the tabloid furore over the movie, *Alien* failed to meet with universal critical acclaim. The cult fantasy periodical *Cinefantastique* was far from stirred. 'As hard as it pretends to be new and stylish, *Alien* is just another bloodthirsty shocker, albeit with a classier production than most ... a highly derivative formula scare show.' The weak plot and ill-defined characterizations bore most of the brunt of the criticism, although the film's technical achievements and entertainment value were much applauded. 'In looks and atmosphere it is a breakthrough for science fiction films in much the same way that *2001* was in its time,' said London's *Evening Standard*.

Sigourney Weaver, however, received unlimited praise for her remarkable début movie performance. *Newsweek* hailed her as the new golden girl of the cinema, with the actress claiming the front cover, which was subsequently framed and hung on her office wall. The English critics were no less impressed with Weaver. The *Daily Mail* called her 'a spectacular new actress and a star of rare distinction'. The *Sunday Telegraph* described her as 'a handsomely wrapped package of grade A talent'. And *Time Out* magazine rated her performance as 'the best screen début in years'. Not only had Sigourney Weaver finally arrived on the international movie stage but, thanks to the worldwide success of *Alien*, she had become a star overnight. But what price success? The making of *Alien* had been fun, to some degree; Sigourney was clearly thrilled to have made her movie début in the leading role; but she did feel that she had been thrown in at the deep end. She had advanced and grown as an actress in the theatre by playing supporting character parts, a successful *modus operandi* which she had hoped to repeat in the movies. This was not to be; from now on Sigourney would be cast and thought of solely as a leading player. But beginning her movie career in a star-making role had still been an exciting experience, if a little confusing and bewildering. Because of Sigourney's limited film knowledge, she was very easy-going on the *Alien* set, despite the difficult atmosphere. Only after filming finished did the actress realize how much strain she had been under. 'I worked terribly hard under conditions I did not think were terribly pro-actor.' Sigourney felt that the technical aspects of the film, the lighting, effects etc. were more important to Scott than the actors, and she blamed the assistant directors for being 'incredibly surly', for reasons she could never fathom. She remembers once seeing a tearful John Hurt in the office of one of the producers, the pressure was that great. 'Everyone said it was the toughest movie they'd ever made,' claimed Sigourney to *Première* magazine in October 1988. 'I never wanted to make another film again.'

5 *Boa Feathers*

Sigourney Weaver wore the mantle of film stardom with a certain amount of unease. Although she felt jubilation about the success of *Alien*, sudden fame was a frightening and odd new experience. After her sensational movie début Sigourney was flooded with letters and presents from adoring fans from all over the world. Even her agent, who had been in the business for many years, had never encountered such adulation before or had so much trouble dealing with people such as those trying to get in contact with Sigourney. One fan, for example, regularly sent her roses, while others would shower her agent's office with lavish gifts which an overworked secretary would always have to return. Sigourney had not anticipated this kind of public response or fan worship. It took her something like a year to finally get around to answering the mountain of mail she had received. On the whole, she was appreciative of the letters which were genuinely sincere and complimentary, but there were the odd few that caused her much distress – letters written by angry or disturbed people, full of pain and internal chaos, demanding instant replies. 'I can't live unless you write to me now,' they would invariably say. 'You're the only person who can understand what I'm feeling.' Sigourney always finds it hard coping with these kinds of letters and doesn't usually respond to them. In today's climate Hollywood stars are fully aware of the danger posed by obsessive or psychotic fans, especially those who seek revenge after being rejected by their favourite idols, their love now twisted by rage and bitter hatred. For Sigourney, living in New York, already a violent city, the added threat of crazed fans represented no real problem or foundation for concern. Sigourney still felt perfectly safe walking the busy, pedestrian-clogged streets, riding on the bus or the subway, and most of the time she went unrecognized. 'There are ways of carrying oneself that will keep you from being noticed.' But occasionally the inevitable happened and she would be followed, an unnerving experience.

Sigourney also found herself suddenly and almost completely cut off from her old acting colleagues. Returning to New York in the wake of her movie début, she found that many things had changed. Nearly all of her friends were still struggling to find work; they couldn't even get walk-on parts in movies or substantial roles in stage productions. Yet Sigourney was now this major new star, the cinema discovery of the year, deluged with appetizing offers of work. 'There was no reason I could define why I was chosen and they weren't,' she said to *City Limits* in October 1988. 'All I felt was: how embarrassing. I'm a success.' She noticed that some of these friends now perceived her in a different light; her success had opened up a huge chasm between them. Sigourney never acted the big movie star on her return, she never snubbed her friends or spurned her old haunts in preference for greener fields. Nor did she move out to Hollywood like so many before her, returning instead to her crummy little flat near the Hudson River. At the same time as *Alien* was reaping in box-office millions around the world and critics were being captivated by Sigourney's performance, the actress lived in a basement apartment close to where the subway trains are coupled. 'It's the most excruciating sound you've ever heard in your life,' she described to *New York* magazine in June 1984, 'Here I was, in a blockbuster and living in a place I equated with hell.' Most significantly of all, Sigourney went straight back to work on the same stages on which she had performed before her *Alien* encounter.

Despite being introduced, by an old friend of her father's, the actor Hume Cronyn, to one of America's biggest agents, Sam Cohn (the New York based agent who has Meryl Streep on his books and respected directors like Mike Nichols and Woody Allen), Sigourney's career did not take off with the prophesied propulsion. This situation was partly of her own making. Instead of solidifying her good fortune by immediately beginning work on another major commercial cinema project, Sigourney turned down numerous film roles

An early publicity portrait of Sigourney as Warrant Officer Ripley – the role that catapulted her to world stardom overnight.

The two very different faces of Lauren Slaughter from the film *Half Moon Street* (1986).

Possessed by evil spirits Sigourney is at her raunchiest as Dana Barrett in this scene from the hit movie *Ghostbusters* (1984).

and returned to the welcoming arms of Christopher Durang and the theatre. Such a decision might have left the actress vulnerable to criticism of her apparently apathetic attitude to offers of film work. 'I've never felt really competitive about movie roles,' she conceded in 1981. This outlook is a legacy from the theatre, where there isn't half as much hostility between actors vying for the same job as there is in Hollywood. On many occasions, Sigourney has been up for a stage role in direct competition with a friend, but this healthy professional rivalry never once affected a personal relationship. Indeed, if she ever lost out to a colleague at least she would know the part was in capable hands. Hollywood is a different matter altogether. So much bitterness exists between performers looking for work, mainly because in Los Angeles the film industry is everything to so many people; 'even your gynaecologist has a script for you,' Sigourney jokes. To be fair, her indifference wasn't nearly as profound as it first appeared. If a movie role emerged that appealed to her, then she would fight like a cat to claim it over anyone else. But too often, when discussing a film role with a casting agent, Sigourney's mind would wander and she'd begin thinking about the actress *she* might cast if the producing reins were in her hands.

Together, Sigourney and Chris Durang resurrected the cabaret *Das Lusitania Songspiel*, which they had written some years earlier. This revival presented Sigourney with ample opportunity to show off her considerable comedy talents, and was a critical and popular off-Broadway hit when it was produced at the Chelsea Theatre. Both participants received Drama Desk nominations for acting and writing. The play featured sketches enacted by the duo in full formal evening wear. Sigourney's send-up of Marilyn Monroe was a particular highlight and often brought the house down. Even the programme notes were a spoof. According to Sigourney's bio she and Durang were married with two children. A nice jest. She skilfully countered the suggestion that one day the two of them would settle down together. 'The relationship is professional, but we're both single, so who knows what may happen ...? We'd have devilish little children if we got married, but I doubt that we will,' Sigourney told a journalist from the *Sunday Telegraph* in June 1983.

The essential reason behind Sigourney's decision to return

immediately to the stage after her initial foray on to the big screen, was the shock and disbelief she felt about the lack of substantial roles for women in cinema. After *Alien*, the actress had naturally assumed that other great parts existed in Hollywood. As a rule, however, it is a man who plays the more interesting characters and around whom the film's plot and situations revolve. This was a disturbing revelation. For a star in the making, Sigourney expressed remarkably bold views on anti-feminism among producers. In the vast majority of the scripts she read women were always on the periphery of the narrative, totally uninvolved in the action, mere ornaments and playthings for the man, whether as wacky girlfriends or the token liberated woman. The film industry *en masse* appeared to be deliberately promoting female stereotypes and wilfully blind to the demands of modern audiences who wanted to see more women professionals on the screen. Films like *Gorillas in the Mist* and *Working Girl* helped enormously to rectify this detestable oversight. Hollywood executives have since learnt not to offer Sigourney scripts in which she's 'a mere satellite to the male lead'. Journalists have also been chided for calling her an actress. 'I'm an actor,' Sigourney proudly proclaims. 'An actress is someone who wears feather boas.' To a large extent *Alien* spoilt Sigourney because she was playing such a strong, interesting woman. 'That's why I didn't work in films for a long time. I was horrified by what they were sending me.'

Despite strong reservations about an *Alien* follow-up and her own admission that 'I wouldn't want to do another sci-fi film anyway', Sigourney remained keen on the idea primarily because, after reading the deluge of scripts sent to her afterwards (most of which were fantasy based), she now appreciated the rare nature of the character she had played. She rejected all of these with the contempt they deserved, although she later admitted that she perhaps should have taken some of them. 'I think early on I attached too much importance to what came next.' Rumoured projects included a film about female athletes to be directed by Robert Towne (famous for writing *Chinatown* and *Shampoo*), and a picture for Richard Attenborough chronicling the exploits of a wartime entertainer in Germany. 'I used to read every script like a college professor.' To prove the point, Sigourney declined a lucrative offer to appear opposite Luciano Pavarotti in his cinema début *Yes, Giorgio*. A wise move; the film turned out to be a complete turkey. Sometimes Sigourney herself was the victim when roles she probably wouldn't have minded playing slipped through her fingers. In one such case she lost the female lead in *Urban Cowboy* to Debra Winger because she was considered too old. Alas, the very role she should have played, Kathleen Turner's seductress in *Body Heat*, was turned down by her agent because he was under the impression that the film's director, Lawrence Kasdan, was a complete pervert. The script was littered with graphic sexual directions 'he goes down on her, she goes down on him', and the like – which he found objectionable. Sigourney's search for a valid and strong female character to play ended when the British director Peter Yates (*Bullitt, The Deep*) offered her the part of TV reporter Tony Sokolow in his romantic thriller *The Janitor*. This was the kind of role she had been waiting over a year to play.

The Janitor (US title: *Eyewitness*) was the second collaboration between director Peter Yates and writer Steve Tesich, the pair responsible for the critically acclaimed *Breaking Away*, for which Tesich had won an Oscar. The story of *The Janitor* originates from Tesich's college days. In his youth the writer spent some of his summer vacations working as a night janitor in Chicago. The memories of eerie evenings alone in those huge, shadowy, empty buildings, where in his own imagination, behind each closed office door innumerable evils were taking place, never left him. He knew that this would one day make the perfect setting for a murder mystery. A few years later Tesich became infatuated with a female television reporter from CBS. He began to speculate to what extremes he would go in order to meet her and declare his passion. From these two separate speculative strands the central character of Daryll Deever, and the film's basic plot, took shape. Daryll (played by that consummate American actor William Hurt), works the late shift as a janitor in a Manhattan office building. He is besotted by top TV journalist Tony Sokolow (Sigourney Weaver), whom he avidly watches every night. On his rounds one evening, Daryll stumbles upon the murdered body of a Vietnamese diamond merchant. This grisly discovery brings him into contact with the woman of his dreams, for it is Tony who is sent to cover the story for television. Daryll seizes his chance to meet her and piques her professional interest by pretending to know more about the murder than he actually does. This reckless action soon puts both their lives in danger. Daryll is disarmingly direct in telling Tony the extent of his love and soon the couple are cavorting between crumpled sheets, after an incident in which Daryll rescues Tony from a gang of kidnappers (a sequence which called for Sigourney to roll out of a moving car and jump on to a getaway motorbike). She performed this stunt herself 'because it told you a lot about the woman'. It tells us a lot about Sigourney Weaver, too. The lack of any great romantic foreplay prior to the love scene suggests that Tony is sleeping with Daryll just to get the story. However, her feelings for the man grow rapidly thereafter. While reading the script Sigourney had doubts about her character's true feelings for Daryll. Only after watching the film did she feel that their romance was genuine. Her love for him blossoms gradually; 'it's as she begins to listen to Daryll as a woman and not as a reporter'.

The success of *The Janitor* hinges on the audience's belief that two diametrically opposed people can fall in love. Daryll is a humble janitor from a tough working class background, while Tony is the privileged daughter of wealthy, cultured parents who are prominent members of New York's élite social scene. (Shades here of Sigourney Weaver's own background.) The Sokolows disapprove of their daughter's career in hard news television and want to see her married to Joseph (Christopher Plummer), a rich diplomat who organizes the exodus of persecuted Jews from the Soviet Union, but who also hides darker secrets. It is doubtful that Daryll and Tony would ever have met under normal circumstances. It took a murder to bring them together. They are from two different worlds, even though they live in the same city. Daryll however, has inbred self-respect and a total disregard for class barriers. This allows him to court Tony, much to the wrath of her parents. Although it is a touch implausible that Tony, with all her material trappings and her polished European Jewish roots, would fall for a man like Daryll, both actors work so well as a couple that they make the fantasy work. 'Hurt and Weaver look great together. Whatever the social differences nature is on their side, they match up,' as the critic from *The New Yorker* remarked. Unquestionably, William Hurt was the most successful and compatible of all Sigourney Weaver's male co-stars. *Time* magazine fancied that after *The Janitor* 'a canny movie producer will want to recast them as the Tracy and Hepburn of the eighties'. Before the film's release there was a general sense of excitement at a product that starred two of America's most promising young, smart screen actors. They were seen to have much in common; each had previously made strong reputations for themselves in the theatre; their acting methods and preparatory work were similar; and both had made their cinema débuts in hi-tech, pretentious fantasy films, William Hurt in *Altered States* and Sigourney Weaver in *Alien*. For both actors *The Janitor* was their second movie. Sigourney enjoyed the experience of working with William Hurt. Every day the two stars would rehearse together, but always mistrusted planning things too much: a scene should never lose its spontaneity. During filming Yates discouraged his actors from improvising, a restriction that Sigourney found difficult to cope with at first. The only time she and Hurt were allowed to use their improvisation skills was in the scene where Tony interviews Daryll for one of her TV broadcasts.

In order to bring maximum conviction and realism to the role of Tony, Sigourney Weaver joined New York's local Channel 5 news team. For three weeks she worked alongside top reporter Aida Alvarez and covered everything from drug busts to a murder inquiry. She found her various assignments thrilling, she was able to get a sense of the long hours a reporter works, and was exposed to the harsh realities of the city in a way that both she and her character would never have been had they stayed within the confines of their families. Sigourney was surprised to find that women were extremely successful as TV reporters, but was disgusted to discover that it was usually the woman who was sent out to cover the more grisly stories. 'I guess the news directors feel that having a "delicate" creature in a tough environment makes for a better show.' During her time with Channel 5, she picked up some valuable television interview techniques, such as how to make your subject relax and open up, a skill she feels women are more skilled at than their male counterparts. The actress also spent a short time in the *Washington Post* newsroom, where the atmosphere, with headstrong reporters ever eager for that big scoop, was similar to that of a hectic TV studio. This hunger for stories was a quality that Sigourney wished to bring to Tony's character. She felt that Tony had become a journalist as a form of escape from a restrictive home life, a rebellious act against her parents and her own pampered upbringing. Sigourney liked the fact that the film looked behind the false, glossy veneer of a contemporary television personality and took a peek at the ferment beneath. Yates also explored the emergence of TV reporters as authentic celebrities whose popularity sometimes rivals that of film and pop stars. It is clear, for example, that Daryll falls in love with Tony's media persona, not the real woman. Tony is a multi-faceted individual. 'She's enigmatic, that's why I wanted to play her.' Other preparations for the role included horse-riding lessons and a course in piano playing. In just two weeks Sigourney could perform Mendelssohn before the camera.

The Janitor was shot entirely in New York. Before filming began the cast enjoyed two weeks of intensive rehearsals. Sigourney was impressed with the Yates/Tesich partnership, in her opinion they made a worthy creative team. She did feel, however, that Tesich's script was a little far-fetched and that the character of Tony was underwritten; the focus of the story rested too much on Daryll. During filming there were several disagreements between the two and a couple of fiery clashes. 'The only thing that kept us friends was that we both had a passion for the film we were making.' Sigourney wanted Yates to wield more directorial influence over the proceedings and bring the film back down to a firmer and more realistic base. She would have liked to have seen more of Tony working in her TV office and have had more details from Tesich about Tony's background, her relationship with her family, why she falls in love with a janitor, and the role that Daryll plays in her life. But Sigourney still applauded Tesich for creating an interesting female character who was involved in most of the film's action. Tony is certainly much more aggressive and ambitious than Daryll, and more successful career-wise – factors that must have appealed to Sigourney.

The Janitor opened in America in mid-March 1981 to a poor box-office reception, a mere $2 million gross. Sigourney was most philosophical about the movie's failure. 'Fox put the film into a computer and the computer spat out that it would do badly, so when the film finally opened small in New York and got good reviews, they were caught without ever having booked it into national theatres. Terrific, eh?' Also to blame was the slump in US cinema admissions. March 1981 was a decidedly poor month; in fact, it was the worst March for ten years in terms of actual ticket sales. The picture fared little better in Britain when it was released on 8 October. Not even the presence of Yates and Tesich at the London press show could save *The Janitor* from box-office death. But the film was greeted favourably by many critics. 'Tense, exciting. Enjoyable entertainment' – The *Sunday Express*; 'Weaver and Hurt are brilliant in an out of the ordinary thriller' – the *Daily Mirror*. Sigourney's best notice for the film came from the *New Yorker* which said, 'Weaver seems a natural for stardom in this era, she's scaled to be a modern heroine.' Despite being away from the screen for almost two years Sigourney's star aura had not diminished. With *The Janitor* she reaffirmed her position as one of the cinema's most exciting new talents, a performer who was able to invest the characters she played with her own charm, warm humour, intelligence and feminist sensibilities.

Regardless of the rave reviews she received at the time, Sigourney dislikes her portrayal of Tony Sokolow. 'All I can see on the screen is how hard I worked,' she related to *You* magazine in May 1983. 'I'm very stiff and that's because I was trying to do too much. After *Alien* I was determined to master film acting and as a result I forgot, or hadn't learnt, to relax.' Relatively unfamiliar with the furious world of cinema, Sigourney found the actual process of movie making by turns anarchic, frustrating and exciting. To her the theatre was a vastly more reassuring environment in which to work. A stage play allowed the actor far more breathing space. One was cast; problems and difficulties were ironed out during rehearsals; and the chance was always there for the actor to keep working on a character, to add new things to the portrayal every performance. By comparison, the movies were crazy and hectic. But film had its virtues. The subtle, intimate moments shared between actors on stage could sometimes be lost in a large auditorium. But film captured these admirably. 'That's one thing I learned from movies. You don't have to hype it up.' Despite misgivings about her own performance, she admired the way the whole cast of *The Janitor* worked together. Unlike *Alien*, they managed to create a cohesive working atmosphere, which Sigourney adored. Perhaps this was because most of *The Janitor*'s cast had worked on the stage previously. Weaver feels that the ensemble idea, to which she earnestly subscribes, is easier for the theatre actor to comprehend.

The Janitor remains an underrated film, an overlooked curiosity. Yates and Tesich failed to achieve the quality of structural and thematic balance of *Breaking Away*; their narrative skills just weren't good enough here to interweave a love story and a melodrama into a satisfying whole; the murder plot was too complicated and needlessly cluttered with minor characters and plot twists. However, the film had a satisfactory air of sophistication about it and was a welcome return to the kind of films that were made forty years before. Indeed, the picture was intentionally photographed in the style of an old Humphrey Bogart movie.

Between the close of filming on *The Janitor* and its eventual release Sigourney Weaver's life was a veritable whirligig of activity. There was an admirable return to the stage in yet another Durang play, *Beyond Therapy*, perhaps his best-known work due to the fact that it was made, unsuccessfully, into a film in 1987 starring Jeff Goldblum and Glenda Jackson. The off-Broadway version was decidedly better and more respectfully received. The play, which seeked to ridicule the psychiatrist and his curious occupation, was presented at the Phoenix Theatre in January 1981. Sigourney played a woman who has a steamy affair with her bisexual analyst. Sigourney's relationship with Durang, born out of the turmoil of Yale, is a true testimony to friendship and talent. Theirs is a strange, yet fruitful partnership; one might even call them the 'odd couple'. But their writing collaborations are proof of how well matched they are. They share the same sense of the bizarre and a love of black, offbeat comedy; both are endowed with an eccentric wit and take a sideways view of the world they inhabit. Their wildest caper occurred in the year of Sigourney's rise to tabloid fame, thanks to her role in *Ghostbusters*. Together they wrote and performed a fine parody of those awful, self-congratulatory celebrity interviews that appear in the glossy magazines. Entitled *The Naked Lunch*, the mock-interview took place at the palatial Russian Tea-Rooms. Sigourney and Durang smeared one another with caviare and printed the result, complete with photographs, in an edition of the *Esquire*. Part of the interview ran as follows:

C.D.: Tell me, how did you get the leading role in *Alien*?
S.W.: I slept with the director.
C.D.: And *Eyewitness*?
S.W.: I slept with the director and the writer and the crew.
C.D.: And *The Year of Living Dangerously*?
S.W.: I slept with the Australian consulate.

The feature proved so popular that Weaver and Durang had plans to write an expanded film version to be made by *Ghostbusters* director, Ivan Reitman. 'We've written some very funny stuff, but we're both so busy and bad and lazy.' In the early years the two of them would spend long days together making each other laugh, cracking jokes, and writing. But as Sigourney grew in stature as a film actress the two old partners had difficulty finding the time for writing sessions. No longer were these spontaneous occasions; now they had to be carefully scheduled in order to fit in with their respective work commitments. Things just weren't the same. In any case, Sigourney now felt the desire to go it alone, to write solo, beginning with short stories, although she still enjoyed the fun and excitement of writing comedy with a partner. It wasn't until the mid-eighties that Sigourney finally treated herself to a word processor. 'I can't believe I put it off for so long,' she told *Cable Guide* magazine in July 1987. 'I thought, "Oh, I don't even write with a pencil, why should I write with a computer?" But I wrote a poem the first day. It was so easy. I'm hoping this will inspire me to do more.'

The most significant new arrival in Sigourney's life in 1981 was a man by the name of James McClure, an actor/playwright whom she had first met during the production of *New Jerusalem* some years before. McClure was currently in the process of getting his play *Lone Star* made into a movie. He had been working for eighteen months on the project. Sigourney found the play interesting and felt strangely drawn to the central female character of Elizabeth. Weaver also found herself captivated by McClure. He was after all a handsome, multi-talented man, and single, too, which helped. In turn he was struck by the actress's beauty and intelligence. It was largely inevitable that the two would get together: they shared similar attributes and common interests, and their mutual love of the theatre led to many happy hours of enjoyment together. A serious love affair soon flourished. Sigourney's past romantic liaisons had gone undocumented, except for her relationship with Aaron Latham, a journalist to whom she was apparently engaged to in her late teens. (Despite Sigourney's demure and refined façade she can sometimes be capable of the most colossal tantrums. One morning, at Latham's New York apartment, the lovers began to argue in bed. Suddenly, Sigourney leaped out from under the covers and ran to the kitchen. She emerged seconds later carrying a carton of eggs which she then proceeded to throw at Latham. The first struck the wall, the second a nearby table lamp, but the third was a direct hit.) Now thanks to the success of *Alien*, the public's desire for scandal and information on this most secretive of new stars was so great that the popular press immediately sprang into action to meet the demand. A New York gossip columnist from the *Daily News* finally got wind of the Weaver/McClure affair and reported that Sigourney had moved out of her basement flat and moved in with McClure at an apartment on Riverside Drive, although they had to leave quickly because the place was infested with bugs. They temporarily moved to the Algonquin Hotel while an exterminator cleaned up the love-nest.

Meanwhile McClure's efforts to get *Lone Star* on film seemed closer to fruition when director Robert Altman (*M*A*S*H, McCabe and Mrs Miller*) became involved in the project and 20th Century Fox agreed to put up the budget. Altman wanted Sigourney in the lead, opposite Powers Boothe, who had been pencilled in as her co-star. For the lovers it all seemed like a dream come true. But fate was later to deal them a cruel hand. The story of *Lone Star* dealt with the tough realities of life for Vietnam war returnees and other legacies of that conflict, a powerful and popular theme among film-makers at the time. Movies like *The Deer Hunter* and *Coming Home* (both 1978) attempted to entertain their audiences whilst patching up the still festering conscience of a nation haunted by the war. In *Lone Star* Sigourney was to play Elizabeth, a 'wonderful, very wry' Texan lady. She loved the part and couldn't wait to bring it to life on the screen. With her customary dedication, Sigourney spent a year preparing for the role. Part of the groundwork included a summer trip to Texas where the actress taped conversations with an assortment of local women. Then, just three weeks before shooting was due to begin, 20th Century Fox pulled out and the project withered, leaving Sigourney devastated and heartbroken. 'I was filled with things I wanted to express as Elizabeth, and I had nowhere to put them, but to throw them away,' she said to *Première* magazine in October 1988. Because Sigourney's first two movies had been made under the auspices of 20th Century Fox she wrongly assumed that, as in the old days of the studio system, the company actually cared about her career and growth as an actress. A naïve thought indeed. This revelation of the callousness of the business side of the movie industry was disturbing. She was shocked that Fox were capable of such an arbitrary decision, seemingly without a care for all the time, effort, and dreaming that had gone into the project. For the first time in her career, Sigourney felt at the mercy of the giant movie conglomerates and the powerful, invisible executives who run them. It was an unpleasant feeling.

Hurt and bewildered Sigourney returned to EST where she tried to make sense of her life and career. She embarked upon the Mastery, a seminar that mainly attracted theatrical types. Here she thought deeply about what could be done in the future to prevent such an event from happening again. Weaver's priority now was to become an actress with whom other people wanted to work. She thought less about attaining fame and fortune and more about the quality of the productions in which she appeared. Perhaps, Sigourney mused, if she worked with the right sort of artists a repeat of the *Lone Star* episode could be avoided. However, if she had been more of a star, with box-office clout and influence, she might have been able to save the project. One doubts that Fox would have cancelled *Lone Star* if Meryl Streep or Jane Fonda had been involved. This realization was the impetus for her to work harder and make more films. It also lent weight to her much vaunted ambition to cross over into the production side of the movie industry, where she could create her own independent pictures free from any outside interference. Even in her early days as a struggling actress in New York Sigourney dreamed of heading west to Los Angeles and becoming a film production assistant. Many established stars (Redford, Beatty, Costner) develop a keen desire later on in their careers to work behind the camera, to direct, produce, or set up their own production companies. But in Sigourney's case this attraction to production was alive in her right from the very beginning of her movie career. As early as 1981, with just two movie appearances under her belt, Sigourney told journalists that she felt it was almost inevitable that one day she would form her own production company. 'I have much of my father's producer in me,' she said. Sigourney was anxious to breathe life into projects and characters that would never have existed without her input, and to create leading roles for actors that she admired but felt were being ignored by the big studios.

For Sigourney the Mastery course at EST was most supportive; it filled an important gap in her life at that time. The Samurai was another course that Sigourney participated in. She attended these morning sessions twice-weekly. Sometimes in class she would sit there, miserable in the knowledge that all the women around her had boyfriends and she didn't. Ironically, one of the girls in the seminar group had a Hawaiian boyfriend at the time, a handsome theatre director called Jim Simpson; Sigourney's future husband. After the course, she once again felt in total control of her life. The Samurai work had made Sigourney realize that although her career was presently in a lull, things weren't as bad as they seemed; she was still incredibly lucky, and unlike many of her contemporaries who were still struggling, Sigourney was a star with a bright future ahead of her. *Lone Star* might have collapsed but at least Sigourney had been entrusted with the leading role. 'What was my problem. I think I've never forgotten that.'

The collapse of *Lone Star* had placed a massive strain on the Weaver/McClure partnership and was a dominant factor in the couple's eventual separation. 'It was a horrendous time which left a lot of wreckage, including our relationship.' But Sigourney managed to survive this particular professional and personal trauma intact, and emerged at the other end leaner and stronger than ever before. Perhaps too strong. Her father was worried that his daughter was becoming obsessive about her career. 'If you're really dedicated to the theatre, that has priority,' Sylvester disclosed to a reporter from *Premiere* magazine in October 1988. 'And it certainly has with Sigourney.' The fact that his daughter had not as yet found a stable partner and settled down was a matter of grave concern. He and Elizabeth had been married now for four decades and neither of them could grasp what Sigourney found so appealing about single life. Sylvester had met McClure on several occasions, later describing him as a 'fun guy', but on the whole, as in the past, he questioned Sigourney's choice of friends. Her close companions were all connected in one way or another with show business; the actress seemed to possess few friends that existed beyond the sphere of entertainment. 'If she's looking for anybody with brains, certainly actors have no brains, by and large,' Sylvester once said. But Sigourney rejoiced in the social side of her chosen profession, the constant round of parties and dinners, the steady flow of new and exciting people to meet. She scarcely felt the need to step out of her gregarious world and search for dates. She eventually reached the point, however, when she suddenly stopped in her tracks and thought, 'Well, I'm successful. Is this it? There must be something more interesting than this,' she revealed to *Interview* magazine in July 1988. Sigourney was lonely after all.

Shaken by the poor public response to her second movie and the *Lone Star* fiasco Sigourney sought sanctuary in her beloved theatre – with disastrous results. In spite of the dire response to *The Janitor*, Sigourney was still rightly hailed as one of the cinema's hottest female properties. Such was her status that she was now in a position to command roles on

Broadway. In the winter of 1981 Sigourney was chosen to play Lady Macbeth, perhaps theatre's greatest ever female role, opposite Nicol Williamson in his own production of Shakespeare's most famous and bankable play. The casting of Sigourney Weaver as Lady Macbeth made headlines across America. *Variety* and the other trade papers reported her signing, even periodicals such as *Newsweek* judged the news important enough to warrant column space. The thought of performing Shakespeare on Broadway was both a daunting and exhilarating prospect for her, but as early as the first week of rehearsals it was obvious that Williamson's and Sigourney's ideas about how Lady Macbeth should be presented clashed violently. Williamson wanted a traditional interpretation, while Sigourney was anxious to make the role more modern. Just ten days before the play's opening night (and what would have been Weaver's Broadway début), the actress walked out of the production. She cited artistic differences with Williamson as her reason. Later, Sigourney admitted that she had been fired. 'I was disappointed', she told journalists, 'because I love the role, and I still want to play it one day.' Her dismissal was a tragedy; she would have made a fantastic Lady Macbeth. In the end the right decision had been made. The only thing tougher than being fired would have been to have played the part night after night under all that pressure. When the news first leaked about Sigourney's sacking the tatty columnists, hot for gossip on the reclusive Weaver, tried to make a headline story out of the incident. But, try as they might to provoke comment no one, not even Williamson, would say anything derogatory about the actress. On the contrary, the crew had nothing but praise for Sigourney; she had been a joy to work with. Nonetheless, the incident left her with a number of bad press reports and she was unfairly labelled as a star who was difficult to work with. Williamson's *Macbeth* production went on to be slain by the critics and was forced to close soon into its run. As for Sigourney, she had a role in a major international motion picture, Peter Weir's *The Year of Living Dangerously* with Mel Gibson, to look forward to.

6 *Living Dangerously*

As Sigourney stepped off the plane at Manila airport on a bright, swelteringly hot day in March 1982, she sensed a spirit of apprehension and danger in the air. The army vehicles that lay scattered around the perimeter of the airport like overgrown and abandoned Dinky toys didn't help to settle her frayed nerves, nor did the spectacle of soldiers armed with submachine-guns, smiling insincerely beneath their helmets. For the average package tourist, or even a visiting Hollywood star, this was hardly a welcoming sight. I myself experienced a similar kind of culture shock on a visit to Rumania, a year before the uprising. As our aircraft approached the meagre terminal buildings I noticed a plethora of war planes and tanks stationed close to the edge of the runway. After our disembarkation we were greeted on the tarmac by a stern-looking soldier brandishing a Kerishnikov rifle. My acquaintance with the communist military machine ended at the airport. Sigourney wasn't so lucky. Even in the secluded privacy of her hotel she felt the presence of the local army. There were armed guards on patrol on every floor, and in the luxury of the hotel lobby Sigourney suffered the indignity of being frisked.

The actress was in the Philippines to make the film *The Year of Living Dangerously* for Peter Weir, a love-story based on the novel by Charles Koch, set during a period of political upheaval in Indonesian history in 1965. During filming, reality began to imitate art rather too closely for comfort and a month after their arrival Sigourney and the rest of the crew were fleeing the country in genuine fear for their lives. Apart from the usual logistical headaches inherent in making a large-scale movie in such a far-flung region of the world there was also the odd unnerving encounter with the local residents. When casting directors went looking for people to play victims in a roadside massacre scene, villagers fled in blind panic. Sigourney was never happy with the choice of the Philippines as a location. Originally Weir had hoped to make the film in Indonesia itself, but his hopes were dashed for technical rather than political reasons. Malaysia also proved to be an unrealistic option. The Philippines had originally been chosen because it was the perfect surrogate location for Indonesia. The authorities in Jakarta had welcomed Weir and his crew. *The Year of Living Dangerously* was the first American film to be made in the country since Francis Coppola's *Apocalypse Now*, four years before.

Sigourney's oriental initiation was a bewildering and disturbing adventure. She found eastern culture and the Filipino way of life fascinating. It was a totally new experience for her, sometimes rewarding, at other times sickening. But she also abhorred the place. Among certain sections of the population she felt very inhibited, particularly in some of the poorer villages around Manila, where locals make unwanted Western visitors very aware of their white skin. The actress could see in their faces the fear of and resentment towards her race. 'A dictatorship. Guns everywhere,' is how Sigourney described the Philippines to *City Limits* magazine in June 1983. 'It was a real education to see government censored newspapers in which you could read what Mrs Marcos had for breakfast.' Plunged into this alien world Sigourney found herself totally confused and lost within the wonder, secrecy and danger of the orient. Her sojourn in the country was an incredible experience. 'It wasn't pleasant; it was very difficult. But it was the most all-encompassing film experience I've had. It was like a roller coaster ... but you felt very alive.' Wandering through the streets and markets of Manila the actress was overwhelmed by the sights, sounds, and smells of south-east Asia and the mysteries of a culture so at variance with her own. She was now more conscious than ever of the strong cultural and economical differences between east and west, the widening gulf between the Third World and her own affluent nation. The advantages that she had known as a child and still enjoyed must have seemed to her a shameful heritage in the

The star trio: Melanie Griffith, Harrison Ford and Sigourney Weaver in the chic New York comedy *Working Girl* (1988).

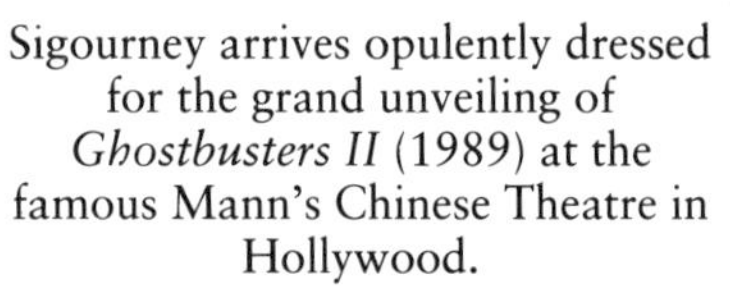

Sigourney arrives opulently dressed for the grand unveiling of *Ghostbusters II* (1989) at the famous Mann's Chinese Theatre in Hollywood.

The actor as victim: Sigourney in one of her least favourite places - a press conference.

A proud Sigourney poses with her parents at the 1986 NATO (National Association of Theatre Owners) gala awards where she was named 'star of the year'.

face of the poverty and suffering that she witnessed all around her in the Philippines. Just like the characters in Weir's film Sigourney felt guilty, and inadequate. She clutched for unattainable answers to the problems facing this part of the world.

Five weeks into a scheduled six-week shoot, filming was progressing normally until one day, while working in a seemingly quiet Muslim village in the Quiapo district of Manila, a member of the crew was sinisterly slipped a note by an anonymous man in the crowd. The note's content sent shock waves through the entire production crew. The letter claimed that Weir's film defamed the local Muslim community and cast a slur on the Islamic world. It finished with the ominous warning: 'Stop your imperialistic acts or we will stop them for you.' Shortly afterwards Sigourney, co-star Mel Gibson, and Weir, all started to receive threatening telephone calls at their respective hotels. Meanwhile, filming on the streets of Manila grew steadily more intolerable as the risk of violence increased. According to one report, Weir was pelted with rocks by some extras during the filming of one scene; at other times outraged citizens would invade the set and hold up filming. Without warning, Weir told his team that they were pulling out within twenty-four hours and returning to Australia. With only minor scenes left to shoot Weir felt he could easily complete the film on replica sets and then carry on with interior filming in Sydney as planned. Both cast and crew breathed a noticeable sigh of relief; the tension in Manila over the past week had become almost unbearable. Apparently, one day during a break from filming Sigourney was approached by a complete stranger and asked if she was afraid of dying. In the words of Gibson: 'It's not worth croaking over a film.' The unit's last night in Manila was nerve-racking, to say the least. They missed their flight out and nervously passed the hours away waiting for another plane in the airport's sparsely furnished lounge, posing as anything but actors in a Peter Weir film.

The mass evacuation of personnel from the Philippines cost the production an extra $250,000 on top of the $6 million budget. But Weir was convinced that this swift action was necessary. In his opinion, the lives of his crew were in danger.

Some cynical journalists claimed that the problems encountered by Weir and co. in Manila was just one big elaborate hoax cooked up by some over-eager PR man in order to garner some valuable advance publicity for the film. The real mystery, however, lies in the fact that a small minority of religious fanatics had been able to scare a major American movie production away from their homeland. How was this allowed to happen? To this day the identity of the culprits is unknown. They could have been any of a number of radical Muslim groups, including the anti-American followers of the Ayatollah Khomeni of Iran. The irony behind the whole incident is that the plot of *The Year of Living Dangerously* had nothing whatsoever to do with the Islamic world, it didn't even tread very deeply into the intricacies of Indonesian politics. The 1965 coup attempt in Jakarta merely served as an interesting backdrop, a canvas on which Weir then painted an elaborate and finely woven tale of intrigue and sex in the tropics. The narrative strives to combine elements of a run-of-the-mill thriller with an unusual love-triangle. The film is really about the cultural differences between east and west, the problems of poverty in the Third World and the west's inability to find any ready solutions.

Guy Hamilton (Mel Gibson), an Australian journalist, arrives in Indonesia on his first overseas assignment to cover the country's precarious political situation. He is appalled by the squalor and the poverty all around him and is repulsed by the indulgences and cynical detachment of his fellow western reporters. Guy finds an unexpected ally in Billy (Linda Hunt), a Chinese-Australian dwarf who arranges an initial news scoop and a meeting with Jill Bryant (Sigourney Weaver), an attaché at the British embassy. The two most beautiful, desirable westerners in town naturally fall in love. But a shadow is cast over their bliss by the imminent threat of civil war. Hamilton becomes embroiled in the political turmoil of the falling regime of President Sukarno, and his dare-devil investigations lead to his inclusion on an assassin's death list. Although Guy is the obvious hero figure the film's soul belongs to Billy: he is its moral core, narrator of and guide to the mysteries and ambiguities of the orient. He is also the controller. Hamilton, however, is everything Billy wishes to be. After Jill spurns Billy's love he orchestrates the affair between the two westerners, (thus saving Jill from lapsing into the embittered cynicism of a failed middle-aged romantic), with the aim of manipulating their destiny. The two lovers are kindred spirits; both care about the squalor and degradation they see. Billy is the ultimate voyeur, akin to the puppet-master of the Javanese shadow-play, the *Wayang kulit*, which opens the film. The puppet motif is central to the work. Choosing the right person to play Billy was Weir's most difficult casting decision. Numerous actors were tested, but all proved unsuitable. Then just three weeks before filming was due to begin, Weir met the New York stage actress Linda Hunt and agreed that she would be perfect for the role. When Charles Koch heard the news that his beloved creation was going to be portrayed on screen by a woman he was furious. But Weir was exonerated when Linda Hunt went on to win an Oscar for her compelling and utterly believable performance as the doomed Billy. The controversial casting of Hunt wasn't the only pre-production clash between Koch and Weir. The writer also disapproved of the way Weir had adapted his novel so liberally and made his protests public in the Australian press. The film's US backers were also given to meddling. Apparently one mogul wanted the film's action transposed to Iran with the Shah standing in for Sukarno.

The Year of Living Dangerously was the first Australian film to be fully financed by a major American company, MGM. Weir was the last of the great new-wave Australian directors, like Fred Schepisi and George Miller, to succumb finally to the lure of Hollywood. Previously he had made films which were very Australian, both in their subject matter and appeal – *Picnic at Hanging Rock*, *The Last Wave* and *Gallipoli*. Weir's track record impressed Sigourney Weaver; she admired the mystical and allegorical elements he instilled into his work. When the director offered Sigourney the part of Jill Bryant she accepted almost immediately, despite the fact that the character was ill-defined and not of central importance to the narrative. So great was her desire to work with Weir that she overlooked her hatred of peripheral roles and plunged in regardless. She knew the film belonged to Gibson and Hunt, she knew her role merely provided some incidental love interest and decoration. But for once she didn't care; this was a small price to pay for the chance of working with one of cinema's great modern directors and she enjoyed the experience immensely. Paradoxically Sigourney seemed to be exercising less control over the material she accepted as her acting career escalated rather than more, mainly because she was now working with a better pedigree of people, stronger directors and classier writers. 'I have to trust their wisdom, their vision. If I was sent a crummy script and a great director was doing it, I'd take it,' she told *American Film* early in 1983. However strong her urge to organize Sigourney admits that she has run her own career on instinct rather than calculation. But for the most part she searched in those early films, in particular *The Year of Living Dangerously*, for stories that took place in the context of larger than life events. Sigourney finds it more interesting to see human beings within a situation that is about something more important than their own identities and relationships. In this respect she was more than willing to take on the relatively minor role of Jill. The point of history that Weir had set his tale fascinated the actress and as she once conceded, 'I'd rather have a small part in a movie I love than a bigger part in one I don't care about.'

Weir was the most demanding director with whom she had yet worked. He didn't want to see acting on the screen, he wanted to see his actors become real people. Weir was also responsible for bestowing upon Sigourney a love of film making that she had never known before. 'What's so philosophically appealing is that you only do it once and its gone – like life.' Sadly, Sigourney only appears sporadically in the film and the character of Jill Bryant is a profoundly flimsy one. But the actress makes the most of what was her first truly romantic cinema role. She looks ravishing, especially in the scene where Jill and Guy are caught in torrential rain while on a date together. Sigourney beautifully conveys an animal lust smouldering beneath the proper and decorous exterior of an English lady. Playing an Englishwoman probably came easier to Sigourney than it would to most other American actresses. 'I'm half-British,' Sigourney once declared with unconcealed pride. 'The good side.' Despite her mother's English roots Weaver still needed the assistance of a dialogue coach during the months of filming, to keep a check on her pronunciation. On Weaver's first day on the set she was approached by a member of the crew who was alarmed at the actress's posh accent. 'Is that the way you talk?' he said. 'Carstle and arsk.' The man was under the impression that Sigourney was one of those snobbish stars who think they are a class above the rest. But she was only practising her English accent before a take.

Sigourney Weaver also enjoyed the experience of working alongside heart-throb Mel Gibson, principally because of the torrid romantic clinches they often had to perform. One steamy moment entailed suggestive fumblings in the front seat of a moving car. In their haste to get into bed the two young lovers defy a curfew and crash their car through a roadblock. 'Of all the crosses an actress has to bear,' recounted Sigourney to *Rolling Stone* magazine in March 1983, 'doing a love scene with Mel Gibson is not one of them.' Likewise, Gibson found Weaver a pleasant companion during filming. 'We had fun together. Never a dull moment.' Despite the two stars' inexperience of love scenes (this was Gibson's first fully fledged romantic role too; Weir had to teach the couple how to kiss for the screen by showing them clips of Cary Grant and Ingrid Bergman from *Notorious*), the dynamism and sexual heat that Weaver and Gibson generated astonished Weir. The director had never anticipated that they would work so well together and had been quite prepared to cut out the romantic subplot if the star pairing had failed. Jill and Guy's affair wasn't a crucial element in the film he wanted to make. In any case, their screen love-affair suffers from being so obviously tacked onto the narrative by Weir. Jill seems grafted on merely to provide Guy with a bit of love interest during lapses in political intrigue, and her bedroom confidences about an arms shipment which point to imminent civil war are only included to present Guy with the journalist's famous dilemma of loyalty versus a story. Amid scenes of poverty, despair, and finally mass bloodletting, a romance seems horribly out of place and shamelessly irrelevant. Weir reduces a terrifying moment in modern history to a glossy backdrop for a couple of well-off westerners frolicking in the sun. After the superbly handled early scenes of hardship and brooding violence, which give the film a hypnotic quality, the love affair is an almost obscene distraction which destroys all tension and reduces the picture to the level of a tame romantic thriller. Weir's final tableau is particularly distasteful. Love conquers all when Guy is reunited with Jill after a romantic dash to the last plane at the airport. He drives through lines of freedom fighters, who have been arrested by the victorious army in its counter-coup, and who provide a final backdrop as they are all systematically exterminated.

Many of those involved in the making of *The Year of Living Dangerously* agreed that it had all the right ingredients to be a massive worldwide hit: an acclaimed and popular director; two rising young stars; a tension-filled story with romantic overtones and exotic locations. In February 1983, MGM hosted a special screening of the movie which was followed by a successful gala reception with a star-studded guest list which included the likes of Charlton Heston and James Coburn. But all eyes were on Mel Gibson and Sigourney Weaver when they arrived together, calm and composed under a storm of popping flash-bulbs. Later in the evening the two stars happily submitted to the horde of photographers who had gathered for the occasion and, at one amusing moment, posed with huge Havana cigars in their mouths.

In May both actors attended the Cannes Film Festival, where *Dangerously* was the official Australian entry for the coveted Palme d'Or, and where it received a standing ovation. They looked radiant and charming together, like an old movie star couple from the forties, as they swanned into a plush cocktail party with the crowd parting in awe and reverence to let them through. Cannes marked a dramatic return to the limelight for the normally publicity-shy Sigourney. The actress makes little contact with the press; she dislikes courting publicity, unless it is to draw attention to a film that she whole-heartedly believes in such as *Gorillas in the Mist*. At Cannes, reporters found Sigourney especially hard to pin down. When the actress did speak out about the film she did so with love and admiration for Weir and her fellow actors. This was no actress going through the motions; she genuinely cared about the film and the character she had played. 'I missed her company for about a year', Weaver later confessed. 'I miss not getting to be with her anymore. I have no reason to, I can't bring her back, I can't call her up.' Sigourney's other promotional duties included a stint on the programme her father created, *The Tonight Show*. One of the producers told Weaver not to think of her appearance as just a plain, ordinary interview, but as a performance. Sigourney didn't disappoint; she entertained the audience by singing 'Row, Row, Row Your Boat' backwards, an old trick she had learned at Ethel Walker. Her other major public appearance that year was at the Oscar ceremony where she co-presented, with Robert Mitchum, the Best Supporting Actress award.

Forgetting the agonies of location filming and her rather subdued role, *The Year of Living Dangerously* is one of Sigourney's favourite movies and one which brought her some of the best critiques of her career. 'Weaver is one of the most potently enticing women I have ever seen on screen' – *Film Directions*; 'She is a compelling film personality, one who brings to a role a distinctive manner that fills a lot of the holes left by the writers' – *New York Times*; and 'Weaver gives her finest performance so far' – *Rolling Stone*. But, despite favourable reviews, the film was a box-office flop on both sides of the Atlantic.

In the space of just five years Sylvester and Elizabeth Weaver had seen their daughter evolve from an accomplished, but overlooked, stage actress into a cinema star of rare quality. She was a superstar in the making. Since his departure from NBC, Sylvester had managed to keep himself busy working on various similar projects. In 1966 he made a short-lived return to network television as executive producer on the revived *Garry Moore Show*. Unfortunately the series failed to pick up satisfactory ratings points and the CBS top brass, ever eager for instant success, fired him. In the early seventies Sylvester moved back into advertising, where he represented clients from all the networks. At the end of the decade he made yet another fleeting return to television. This time he was involved with a late-night pilot show called *The ABC Comedy News*. Later, he was a creative force behind a cable company who planned to form a network service to run programmes of special interest to people over fifty. Sylvester also put his wide-ranging skills to good use for the Disney corporation on their experimental new project, EPCOT, the city of the future, which was then under development at Disneyworld in Florida. Despite the wide variety of jobs, Sylvester's true talent, that of television programming, was never again significantly exploited.

From an early age, Sigourney worshipped her father. One might say that she has been on a personal mission to redeem Sylvester's lost glory. Her relationship with her mother has ostensibly been less agreeable. The two of them would often argue or attempt to score points off one another. Sigourney was also not averse to screaming at Elizabeth. But there was nothing abnormal in that; their relationship was close to the ordinary mother–daughter rivalry. But Sigourney's respect for her father is bottomless and to some extent she carries and shares the pain of his mistreatment at the hands of NBC. 'It just galls me. Everyone bends over backwards to acknowledge my father,' she told *Première* magazine in October 1988. They'd rather acknowledge him than give him a job.' And so it was with a great deal of pride, tinged with a modicum of resentment towards the business which had so cruelly spurned his services, that Sigourney, looking resplendent in a Norma Kamali dress, attended the 1983 Emmy Awards. For the Weaver family this was to be a special night. Sylvester was to be honoured with an award for his great years of service with NBC. It was much appreciated, but some twenty-five years too late. His acceptance speech was a mocking one. He accused the industry of being adrift in a sea of mediocrity. His views found many favourable ears and he left the podium to deafening applause. As the television camera panned the audience it stopped briefly upon the face of an emotional Sigourney. 'Thank you,' she mouthed.

7 *I am Comedy*

In the summer of 1982, Sigourney was back in New York, meeting with old friends and catching up on the new plays that had opened. The Philippine ordeal was now pushed firmly into the past as she eagerly prepared for her return to stage acting. Thanks, in part, to Peter Weir, Sigourney had now developed a keen passion for the process of film making, but her first love was still the theatre and she missed the atmosphere and buzz of a live audience. Weaver was asked to appear at the Berkshire Theatre Festival in Stockbridge, Massachusetts, in the comedy *The Animal Kingdom* by Phillip Barry. Sigourney was paid around three hundred dollars a week but the money wasn't really important, she was so glad to be back in the theatre that she would have performed at the festival for nothing. Later in the year Sigourney returned to the cinema and began work on what at the time seemed a promising and worthwhile venture, *Deal of the Century*. The film was a black comedy which sought to take a harsh and satirical look at one of the most repellent of modern industries, the multi-billion dollar world of the arms dealer. But despite its admirable intentions the movie was a dud in every department. The critical and commercial failure of *Deal of the Century* proved especially puzzling when one considers the high-calibre film making personnel involved – director William Friedkin (*The French Connection, The Exorcist*), screenwriter Paul Brickman (director and author of *Risky Business*, the film that launched the career of Tom Cruise), and producer Bud Yorkin.

To Sigourney her participation in *Deal of the Century* represents an important and progressive step in her career, because at last she was given the opportunity to play film comedy. And comedy, she and many of her working colleagues feel, is her greatest strength. 'She's like Kay Kendall,' said Christopher Durang. 'Beautiful and willing to be sublimely silly. But she's also good at playing comedy for real instead of for easy laughs.' After the serious *The Year of Living Dangerously*, and those tough weeks on location in the Far East, Sigourney hankered after lighter movie projects. She desperately wanted to make a screwball comedy, in much the same vein as those Katharine Hepburn, an actress she admires, had appeared in during the 1930s. Sigourney's ambition to be a film comedienne and take part in a slapstick movie was so great, like her desire to work with Weir, that she willingly succumbed to such undemanding and trite material. She was quite happy to play another peripheral character. The role of Mrs DeVoto is drawn with a thin brush indeed; she is a one-dimensional character scarcely equal to Sigourney's considerable acting abilities. But the role had one important attribute: it was completely different from the kind of 'upscale, refined Bryn Mawr' ladies that Sigourney felt she was constantly being typecast as. DeVoto was an amoral, manipulative bitch, a far cry from the classy, wholesome women Sigourney had portrayed in her last two films.

From the beginning of her cinema career, Sigourney had been desperate to dispel the myth that she could only play serious people, or tough, independent modern heroines. 'For some reason US audiences think I'm some kind of sophisticated rich bitch. I like being funny.' Many cinemagoers were totally oblivious to the fact that most of Sigourney's pre-*Alien* theatre work had been comedy based. She had even gained something of a reputation off-Broadway as a mimic as well as a fine actress, with comedy impressions of Jill Clayburgh and Marisa Berenson for which the *New York Times* called her 'a fine, loose, knockout comedienne'. (Sigourney has always felt more at home playing comedy, like Irene Dunne, one of her favourite actresses, who worked in musical comedy and was always at her best in 1930s screwball farces) 'I want jokes,' declared Sigourney to *Films and Filming* in November 1981. 'Also I'd like to sing and dance in movies.' There is so much potential and talent in Sigourney that has, as yet, been untapped by Hollywood. Her eagerness to show off her comedy skills and to prove that she could be an able film comedienne was apparent from the first day of shooting *Deal of the Century*. 'Boy I'm glad I'm doing this movie,' she confided to her co-star Chevy Chase one morning during rehearsals. 'Nobody knows I play comedy. I'm comedy. I'm telling you, I'm comedy.' Unfortunately, because the picture dealt essentially with a serious subject, admittedly in a light-hearted way, Sigourney wasn't called upon to deliver much zany material. 'She can play comedy though,' Chase confessed to *Interview* magazine in November 1983, following the close of filming. 'There's no question about it.'

Eddie Muntz (Chase) is a small-time arms dealer to the Third World. By chance, he becomes the middleman between a Central American dictator called General Cordosa and Luckup Industries, a massive US defence contractor, in the sale of the Peacemaker, a futuristic, computer-controlled, pilotless fighter plane. To pull off the deal, which is worth some $300 million, Nuntz enlists the help of his partner Ray (Gregory Hines). Sigourney plays a sultry widow, intent on getting her hands on half the loot. The film culminates in a flurry of special effects when the Peacemaker goes haywire at an armaments fair and begins to attack the horde of assembled military men and arms dealers. The film-makers based this sequence on an actual incident which took place in 1981, when a mega-buck remote-controlled anti-aircraft tank went berserk during a test and began firing its missiles at the invited audience. Filming began on *Deal of the Century* on 1 November 1982 in and around the Los Angeles area and at Santa Barbara airport. All interior scenes were shot at the Burbank studio. Friedkin had been promised aircraft and other military hardware by the Pentagon. But when a top-ranking army official read the script he was so outraged by its contents that all assistance was withdrawn. Sigourney was bitterly disappointed; she had hoped to steal a ride in the back seat of a fighter plane. Principal photography finished in mid-January. Sigourney's final scene was a frenetic one: she had to be chased around the arms show by the lecherous General Cordosa. Prior to the take Sigourney ran through a methodical set of limbering-up exercises – she jumped on the spot like a boxer, did a series of knee bends, hyperventilated for a couple of seconds and finally massaged her face. Later in the day she joined her co-stars Chase and Hines who were posing for some publicity stills. The film was almost over, the next day would be the last. When the photo session was over Sigourney yelled, 'I'm free,' and did a fine cartwheel on the astroturf. 'Until tomorrow,' she added. But then it started, the self-doubt that succeeds any finished performance. The worrying. At these times Sigourney remembers what the director Peter Weir told her, words of advice which she classes as the most important lesson she has ever learned in films. 'He said, "You have to have the generosity not to care. Once you've done your part, you have to leave it to them." ' ('Them' being the film makers). Sigourney's part in *Deal of the Century* is distressingly small; she swans through the picture as a chic presence, a decorative foil for the laconic antics of Mr Chase. But in the end she does manage to bring a certain degree of substance to an underwritten role. She told reporters after filming, that DeVoto had been 'the most fun part I've ever had'.

Deal of the Century was released in America in November 1983 in the wake of the success of another Chase vehicle *National Lampoons Vacation*. Unfortunately *Deal* was greeted less tumultuously by the American people. Reviews were harsh. 'It's terrible,' reported *The New York Times*. *New York* magazine complained vehemently: '*Deal* is of an appalling badness rarely encountered in a big budget film made by an experienced director.' Friedkin's only solace lay with the views of *The Motion Picture Product Digest*: 'Not since Kubrick made *Dr Strangelove* has a major film maker used satire on the screen in such a devastating and blistering way.' Financially, the film was an embarrassing flop, a mere $4.5 million in takings to offset a $15-million budget. This was Sigourney's third failure in a row. But in spite of its less than positive reception the actress admits to being fairly fond of the movie, mainly because everybody kicked it so brutally.

Deal of the Century is very much an anti-war film. There are morals aplenty amidst all the jokes and quick-fire visual gags. The sick irony that most of these weapons are designed and sold for peace-keeping purposes is the film's most thought-provoking statement. In the movie the slogan for the arms show reads 'Arms for Peace'. The companies, these purveyors of death, manufacture and sell such weapons merely to keep the world insecure and themselves rich. 'Had the film worked', Sigourney feels, 'it would've been a very nasty satire on the pervasive attitude about arms in the US.' But it didn't. The movie is devoid of artistic merit and comic greatness. Although the basic premise is sound, the direction is muddled. The denunciation of the arms business is no more than a scattershot caricature and the majority of the comedic situations are second-rate. Some of the gags are Hollywood surplus stuff. We are expected to laugh hysterically at such old-hat sights as a Central American dictator's palace overrun with clucking chickens, a Laurel and Hardy inspired tit for tat routine, and a scene in which Cordosa's failure to make love to Mrs DeVoto is intercut with stock footage of aborting rockets and misfiring missiles. Intermittently entertaining, Chase is always pleasing to watch, but the action has all been seen and done before, only better. Warner Bros. didn't even bother to release the film in Britain. *Deal of the Century* finally premièred in the UK on video early in 1985, joining a worryingly long list of supposedly major Hollywood films bypassing the cinema.

Ever since Yale, Sigourney has been in near-constant battle with two aspects of her own persona – her class and her intermittent ambivalence towards her chosen profession. She has gone through phases where she has felt less than devoted to acting. Directly after Yale she was possibly at her lowest ebb, with severe doubts about carrying on. This was a dilemma that re-emerged after *Alien*. The situation reversed dramatically when shooting closed on *Deal of the Century*, which she had made almost directly after *The Year of Living Dangerously*. Suddenly, she was brimming over with enthusiasm; there was a fresh determination in her, a newborn longing to contribute more to film. By making these two pictures back to back, Sigourney had developed a valuable confidence within the cinematic medium. She was now ready to try for superstardom. So strong was the urge to find more movie work and suitable roles to play that she flew to England at her own expense to try and persuade Fred Zinnemann to cast her as Kate in his new production, *Five Days One Summer*, the veteran's first film for over four years. The role of a young 1930s woman on holiday in the alps, hopelessly lost in an affair with a married man twenty-five years her senior, would present Sigourney with numerous acting challenges, and the prospect of working with the director of *High Noon* and *A Man For All Seasons*, and star Sean Connery, filled her with longing. But alas Zinnemann thought her quite inappropriate. Unruffled, Sigourney proceeded to look elsewhere for her next job. She tried out for the role of a chorus girl in Francis Ford Coppola's *The Cotton Club*: 'a kind of Brechtian whore, sexy and savvy'. But she was turned down. She has never been afraid to strike out independently in her search for suitable movie projects and interesting characters to play. This policy is not followed by the great majority of her fellow film actors, who tend to leave that kind of work and hard graft to their agents. But if a part comes along that Sigourney is intent on playing she'll campaign long and hard for it. Many stars of her stature wouldn't even consider such a drastic course of action. 'I've seen some of those campaigns that have been unsuccessful,' Sam Cohn told *Première* magazine in October 1988. 'They've been wonderfully waged with a lot of guts and courage. And when they're lost, she's very hurt. She's unusually sensitive.' But Sigourney hides it well. She masterfully suppresses her emotions beneath a veneer of cool, controlled intelligence. Some people have seen through her, however. Chevy Chase was one, commenting after working with her on *Deal of the Century*: 'She is tense and high-strung. I think one gets the feeling that she could explode at any point.'

Sigourney's search for suitable film projects and characters reached a crisis point in mid 1983. Of all her films thus far only *Alien* had been a hit. The rest were miserable box-office failures, in spite of her acclaimed performances. Since her sensational début the actress had played a variety of interesting women, but all had met with an indifferent response from the public. Audiences around the world still only knew her as Ripley. Even worse, she had been unable to capitalize on her early fame. She had within her grasp a rare shot at stardom. Sigourney desperately needed a hit to re-establish her box-office credibility. Little did she know that her very next project was destined to become one of the most popular movies in cinema history.

8 *The Thinking Man's Sex Symbol*

Conceived by Dan Aykroyd, *Ghostbusters* arose from the comedian's interest in the supernatural, which dates back to his childhood. Aykroyd's family has a history of close encounters with the paranormal; an old farmhouse in Canada, where he grew up, was the scene of many family seances and unexplained psychic disturbances. While writing the first draft of the *Ghostbusters* script Aykroyd drew upon these experiences, and also researched extensively into case-studies of hauntings. The initial screenplay took several years to develop and was intended as a vehicle for himself and his close friend, the late John Belushi. Czech-born Ivan Reitman was approached to direct the film and instantly recognized its potential. The first major problem Reitman had to overcome was Aykroyd's script which was set in the future with teams of ghostbusters competing against each other, and had ghosts and ghouls on virtually every page. It was a sci-fi blockbuster which would have cost upwards of $100 million to realize. Reitman was influential in shifting the emphasis from way-out fantasy to broader comedy. He decided to set the film in present-day New York with the ghostbusters as normal guys who can be called out like firemen to deal with ghosts and other hostile spirits.

The story concerns a trio of zany, but supremely intelligent, scientists: the fast-talking, womanizing Venkman (Bill Murray); the warm-hearted and childishly enthusiastic Stantz (Dan Aykroyd); and Spengler (Harold Ramis), the real brains behind the outfit. On losing their research grant, the three are kicked out of university. They immediately set themselves up in business as ghost exterminators just as New York is innundated by a plague of phantoms and monsters. Working from an old abandoned fire station, their success in hunting down and capturing the city's ghost population leads to fame and fortune. Although it is a unique picture, the origins of *Ghostbusters* date back to the forties and those old black and white comedy scare-movies which invariably starred Abbott and Costello or Bob Hope. Aykroyd cleverly managed to update this genre by combining two of the most popular Hollywood products of the eighties – the college humour of *National Lampoon/Saturday Night Live*, and state-of-the-art special effects.

Sigourney Weaver plays cellist Dana Barrett who seeks advice from Murray and his wacky team after a bizarre supernatural experience in her kitchen. Dana's high-rise apartment block turns out to be the gateway to another dimension from where a primeval god intends to wreak havoc upon the world. Only the ghostbusters stand in its way. The pivotal role of Dana was the last major character to be cast. By the time Sigourney was considered, numerous actresses had already been rejected. From the outset Reitman wasn't keen on Weaver taking on the role, he thought she was too serious a performer to want to play a character who becomes demonically possessed, turns into a red-hot siren and finally a terror dog. However, Sigourney was most enthusiastic. At her interview she joked to the director, 'Ivan, multiple schizophrenics are my speciality.' She was desperate to take part in *Ghostbusters*. With the exception of *Deal of the Century* all her movies had been a bit on the serious side; she now craved a change of image and the chance to take another crack at film comedy. The idea of playing a woman who is taken over by an evil force also appealed to her. It would be an interesting acting exercise to try and summon up her dark side. During her audition she performed the possession scene for Reitman. Midway through her recital she seemed to lose control and began jumping around the couch and eating the pillows. Reitman was shocked, but he gave her the part. The opportunity of acting alongside some of America's most popular and gifted modern comedians was a further enticement. 'I suspected the work would be loose, crazy and spontaneous. And it was. I've done improvisation on the stage, but never before so much and so often in front of the camera.' Numerous scenes were rewritten by the actors themselves and there was much on-set improvisation, most of which was encouraged by the writers. According to Rick Moranis, one of the supporting players, the script was just a blue print and was frequently thrown out. Weaver thoroughly enjoyed working with the comics and hoped one day to make another movie comedy with them all (not necessarily *Ghostbusters 2*), with Reitman at the helm. 'There was so much laughter on the set,' Sigourney told *Starlog* magazine in the summer of 1984. 'Working on *Ghostbusters* was glorious.'

Filming began in October 1983 in New York City. Numerous location sites were utilized, including the New York Public Library, Columbia University, and City Hall. The crew's month-long stay in the Big Apple was meticulously pre-planned. But the shooting of the film's climactic scene almost brought Manhattan to a complete standstill. The search for a suitably baroque building to represent 'Spook Central', the home of Dana Barrett, brought the crew to 55 Central Park West. The long and complicated sequence incorporated a thirty car motorcade, a mini-earthquake, assorted stunt work, and more than 300 extras. Although the streets around Central Park were left more or less clear the normal flow of rush-hour traffic was inevitably disrupted, resulting in long tailbacks of irate drivers sounding their horns in blind protest.

Moving to Los Angeles, work continued on the film's most imposing set, a Babylonian temple situated on top of Dana's apartment block. Built on stage sixteen of the Burbank studios at a cost of $1 million, the set was one of the biggest ever seen in Hollywood. The temple set was logistically awesome. It was sixty feet high, required 3,000 man-hours to build, and drew enough electricity to power a small town. When the set was in full operation all the other stages at Burbank had to shut down temporarily. Less impressive, but equally important was the ghostbusters headquarters (in reality an old fire station right in the middle of Los Angeles' Skid Row, where drunks and other assorted unfortunates are a common sight). So precarious was this location that no one dared leave the set except in the company of others. The irony of making a $30 million movie in an area of abject poverty and hopelessness was not lost on any of the actors.

Ghostbusters was clearly a film that relied heavily on

special effects. The man chosen to co-ordinate them was multiple Oscar winner Richard Edlund, formerly of Industrial, Light and Magic where he worked on such blockbusters as *Raiders of the Lost Ark* and the *Star Wars* trilogy. When Reitman heard that Edlund was leaving the George Lucas stable and setting up his own effects studio the director immediately hired him. Edlund's toughest assignment was creating the weird menagerie of ghosts and creatures that inhabit the film. The most popular and enduring was Onionhead, a green blob with an insatiable craving for food. Mixed in with all the hilarity are a few genuinely scary moments. These are mostly provided by the terror dogs, gruesome creatures that guard a demonic shrine. Unquestionably, the effects highlight is the scene featuring Mr Stay-Puft, a one hundred-feet high marshmallow man brought to life by the demon god in an effort to destroy the ghostbusters.

The film's incredibly intricate and elaborate effects made quite an impression on Sigourney. The actress has always enjoyed the world of special effects and feels safe in the capable hands of filmdom's technical wizards. During filming Sigourney found time to visit Edlund's effects workshop, situated on an industrial park near the famous, but sadly now desolate, Culver City studios. 'That's where they used to make movies,' said a forlorn Sigourney Weaver to *Film Comment* in June 1984 pointing to a landscape of empty and idle soundstages, once the home of MGM and where, amongst other films, *Gone With the Wind* was made. 'Now it's a ghost town.' Sigourney herself was involved in quite a few elaborate live-action effects scenes. In one gripping sequence she is attacked by three demonic hands that sprout from a chair. She proved to be an enthusiastic victim. At first the puppeteers who operated the arms were afraid of hurting the star and were too tame in their efforts to grab hold of her. In the end Sigourney had to forcibly encourage them to get tough and slap her around much harder. Unable to move, a captive of these brutish arms, the chair, as if possessed itself, swivels around, sending the hapless Dana Barrett crashing into the kitchen where the forces of darkness await her. Sigourney found responding to physical threats, such as the arms, relatively straightforward. What was profoundly more difficult was reacting to something, a ghost for example, that was to be added on to the film at a later stage by the special effects experts. In one scene Dana opens a fridge only to find an apocalyptic vision before her. On the day this sequence was shot Reitman had to scramble into the fridge, along with a camera, and when Sigourney opened the door he shouted at her to act scared. One wonders how she was able to keep a straight face. 'It's very hard to act really frightened when you don't have something really frightening to react to. On *Alien* it was a lot easier, because everything we saw was real and all of the effects happened right in front of us.' One effect that was all too real was the levitation. While possessed, Dana Barrett levitates four feet above her bed, much to the nonchalant bemusement of Venkman. To achieve this illusion Weaver was forced to wear a very tight fibreglass body shell which, by means of a concealed rod, moved the wearer up and down. It was an arduous but enjoyable experience. The most dangerous effect involving Sigourney was in the scene where Dana greets a multitude of spiritual forces and an entire wall of her apartment is blown out in front of her transfixed form. Although the wall was made out of harmless balsawood bricks and breakaway glass the actress was still a touch apprehensive and wisely made sure that everything was safe before the cameras rolled. Once reassured, Sigourney put in a couple of earplugs, and was told to stand seven feet away from the danger area and not move a muscle or even blink an eyelid. After the explosion she was covered in debris. 'It was great. I'd love to do it again,' Sigourney told *Cinefex* magazine in the summer of 1984. 'It was just like being behind a tidal wave or being the only person in the world inside an explosion.'

Ghostbusters opened in America on 8 June 1984, following a devastatingly successful four-month advertising campaign. In February a friendly looking white ghost peering through a red circle with a diagonal line through it appeared for the first time on one of those huge billboards that grace Sunset Boulevard. The title of the film was not mentioned; the copy read only: 'Coming to save the world this summer'. This logo soon began to appear all over America: in subways, on prime-time television, in newspapers, and proved to be both eye-catching and memorable. It needed to be, for

Ghostbusters was opening up against big competition in the form of *Indiana Jones and the Temple of Doom, Star Trek III* and *Gremlins*. Happily for all concerned the film surpassed even Columbia's high expectations. In its opening weekend *Ghostbusters* grossed $13 million and went on to earn an astronomical $128 million in America alone, making it the biggest hit of the year and one of the most successful comedy movies in history. By the end of 1984 *Ghostbusters* had entered the all-time box-office top ten. The most hyped movie of the mid-eighties, the film led to a huge boom in related products such as toys, games, clothes, and even a cartoon show. America had gone *Ghostbusters* crazy and the world soon happily followed suit. The film opened in Britain just in time for the Christmas holidays and was a massive hit, the second most popular movie of the decade in UK cinemas. But critically *Ghostbusters* was mauled and Sigourney's performance was generally overlooked. 'Spare a tear for Weaver whose fate it is to appear in ever bigger blockbusters playing ever more cypher-like roles' was a rather damning criticism from *Time Out* magazine.

Sigourney's participation in the smash hit *Ghostbusters* helped revitalize her career; not since *Alien* had the actress amassed so much hype and publicity. Once again her face was staring out from periodicals on paper stands across the nation. This time she was not Ripley, staring blankly at the camera, her face clean of make-up, her body wrapped in a dirty, workmanlike boiler suit, and with a malevolent extra-terrestrial breathing down her neck. This time she was ... the glamorous Dana Barrett sporting an erotic red dress and striking a seductive pose, her face heavily made up. She looked like a technicolour Helmut Newton fantasy. *Ghostbusters* was the first film really to exploit Sigourney's sexuality. Previously, she had been decorous and alluring, particularly in *The Year of Living Dangerously*, but never an erotic force. Suddenly here she was playing a sex siren and having a ball. Never since has her sex appeal been so ravishingly displayed on film. *Cinefantastique* magazine had only praise for her: 'The epitome of class and delectability, Weaver smoulders across the screen in her best role since *Alien*.' And fashion-bible *Harper's Bazaar* voted her one of America's ten most beautiful women. Blessed with intelligence, Sigourney is conscious of her own sensuality, and is in full control of it. But her reaction to the label of sex symbol following her *Ghostbusters* role was a mixed one. 'I'm not really in touch with being a ... er sex goddess,' she admitted to the *Sunday Express* in December 1984. 'I'll have to work on that.' But Sigourney did intend to use this imposed image as a way of removing the last vestiges of her upbringing and class, which she had been trying to escape since her teenage years. For a film star in the 1980s this battle was more crucial than ever, especially if Sigourney was to mature and develop as an actress. Producers were still, relatively speaking, blind to the fact that Sigourney was capable of playing a variety of women from high class ladies to bums and sluts. There are those, however, who believe that subconsciously at least, Sigourney may always retain traces of her privileged childhood and class status. One observer on the set of *Deal of the Century* recalls: 'Whatever Sigourney says she does carry her upbringing around with her. She can be quite demanding, expecting things to be done for her, the "star treatment", not because she thinks of herself as a star, but simply because she's always been used to people doing things for her.' As Sigourney's film career began in earnest she wanted to steer away from playing high-class sophisticates. A constant ambition of Sigourney's has been to confound expectations, to play *femme fatale* parts, Garbo-type roles, or women from the wrong side of the tracks. 'I would love to play a real tart,' she once revealed. 'Some blonde bombshell.' Once a director told her agent that he felt she was just too Bryn Mawr (the austere Pennsylvania girls' college that had spawned Katharine Hepburn), a remark that deeply upset the actress. Her social class has always been an obstacle, however. From those earliest forays into film onwards, producers and directors strove to promote Sigourney as cool and elegant, a woman always in control. She fought hard to win the chance to play against type, to convince those people that just because she had been to Stanford and Yale and had a masters degree, that didn't mean she couldn't play a bum or a slob. 'I'm not too smart to play a slut. But people in this business feel threatened by even minimal intelligence.'

A fantasy object to many, the thinking man's pin-up, Sigourney has never seen herself as someone who sells sex on screen. She finds it distressing watching women forced into playing roles, written by men, which are so obviously a stimulant for a largely male audience. She prefers to see women behaving autonomously or for the benefit of other women. Sigourney admires European actresses like Greta Garbo and Marlene Dietrich, whose genius lay in combining intelligence with sexual allure. However, she judges America's Louise Brooks to be the sexiest woman in the history of cinema: 'Her eyes were a furnace.' Curiously, some months before embarking on her siren role in *Ghostbusters*, Sigourney got the chance to explore her own sexual identity when she agreed to do a photo session with Helmut Newton for *Vogue*. Ever since watching Sigourney exude feminine machismo in *Alien* Newton had wanted to photograph the actress. At first the atmosphere was tense between the two artists. Newton, famous for treating his models like brainless bimbos, mere dolls to operate and position, was quickly made to feel ill at ease once he realized that Sigourney wanted to contribute some ideas of her own. In Newton's world models didn't think, they just posed; they certainly never created concepts for a shoot: that was his job. Originally Newton wanted Sigourney to pose for a lay-out about a Hollywood star, but the actress expanded on this idea and came up with the interesting notion of creating a history of film montage.

Many of Sigourney's friends regarded her decision to be photographed by Newton as an act of madness. She was a serious actress: how could she allow herself to be turned into so much designer clay, putty in the hands of Newton? Sure enough, standing in front of a western backdrop, amply filling a tight mini-dress, a Madonna-style crucifix around her neck and a veil over her face, Sigourney did feel slightly stupid and a little exploited. Newton had made her into an object of desire. By the end of the first day both artists were on the verge of abandoning the whole idea. 'I'm not having any fun,' she declared to Newton. 'You're having all the fun.' Unusually for Sigourney she had arrived ill-prepared for her encounter with Newton. The actress was woefully unfamiliar with the master's art. That night in her room at the Beverley Wilshire Hotel Sigourney looked at a selection of Newton's photographs for the first time and found them 'beautiful, and bizarre and very funny'. She returned the next day in a new frame of mind, ready to deal with being controlled. For the next two days Sigourney found a way to act the role of the archetypal Newton mannequin. By the end of the shoot she was revelling in it. The assemblage of outfits and poses was surreal in its imagery. Newton took some shots of Sigourney in a leather bikini, holding a riding whip, and standing on a mountain of film cans spewing their celluloid. Another shot had her dressed as a man looking at himself as a prostitute in the reflection of a mirror. Some pictures were taken on the Warner Bros. backlot. In one pose Newton beautifully captures the vulnerable figure (dressed in a black skirt slit thigh-high on one side, revealing black garters on flesh), with the lengthening shadows of soundstages and the hills of Burbank behind her. In common with most of Newton's models, Sigourney's face is ashen white, her cheekbones are accentuated, her body writhes in inner passion, her eyes half close in some imaginary ecstasy. So successful was the professional union between artist and model that both were keen on working together again on another photo shoot. But Newton agreed that next time he would concentrate on *Sigourney*'s fantasies.

After *Ghostbusters* Sigourney was one of the most recognizable and popular stars in the cinema. But instead of strengthening her renewed box-office standing and looking for another movie project with wide audience appeal, she did her old *Alien* trick, immediately returning to the theatre. But this time things were different; Sigourney was finally to get her chance to perform on Broadway. The play, David Rabe's *Hurlyburly*, was well worth the long wait and was a mighty success, greatly enhancing her career and reputation as an actor. *Hurlyburly* boasted an impressive cast, the cream of young American acting talent: Christopher Walken, Harvey Keitel. Little wonder the play was so popular with the public. The one overriding joy for Sigourney was the opportunity the play afforded her to work with William Hurt again, but on the stage and in front of a live audience every night this time. The actors had become close friends since the days of *The Janitor* and had cultivated a mutual admiration society for one another's talents, which helped enormously on stage. Almost immediately they managed to build a good rapport and there was a chemistry that made their scenes together that much more special. This shared buoyancy allowed both performers ample freedom for experimentation and gave them the courage to play their scenes as many different ways as they dared. Consequently, their moments on stage were always fresh and stimulating, especially during the comedy scenes. 'We were a funny couple,' Sigourney remembered. So pleasurable was their theatrical partnership that she expressed a burning desire to make a second film with Hurt, or to do another play, either comedy or Shakespeare. 'Basically I'd do anything with Bill,' she said. 'It's fun to work with him.'

Hurlyburly was directed by Mike Nichols, one of the few contemporary American directors able to inhabit the two very different worlds of theatre and film. His theatrical forays tend to be overshadowed by his cinema achievements: *Who's Afraid of Virginia Woolf?*, *The Graduate*, and *Silkwood*. But the man who made his début as a Broadway director with the première of Neil Simon's *Barefoot in the Park*, and followed that up a year later with Simon's masterpiece *The Odd Couple*, is to be respected eternally. Which other director could have persuaded America's foremost comedians Robin Williams and Steve Martin to perform *Waiting for Godot* in 1988, in a relatively small New York theatre? Given his background and reputation, it was little wonder that Sigourney was keen to work with Nichols. But the experience, though ultimately a gratifying and exhilarating one, was demanding and quite painful. In *Hurlyburly* Sigourney played Darlene, a bit of a Hollywood bimbo, who becomes trapped in the perverse games played by two misogynist men. Rabe's play is about the degradation of women and the deep mistrust that exists between the sexes, a theme that had to be explored during rehearsals. This led to an unhealthy and less-than-pleasant working atmosphere. From the beginning, Nichols joked that women were going to be given short shrift in rehearsals. True to his word, Nichols spent the majority of the day working with his male actors: Sigourney and co. were relegated to an hour's rehearsal at the end of the day. Even more insulting was that Nichols persisted in referring to the actresses as niggers. 'That was the status of women in the world of *Hurlyburly*,' says Sigourney.

After he finished with Hurt and the other men, Nichols would announce, 'And now for the niggers.' One wonders just how Sigourney managed to tolerate this.

Although Rabe's work depicts a world in which women are very much second-class citizens and potential victims, Sigourney worked hard to try and make Darlene less of a casualty than Rabe had intended. 'I think maybe I wronged the play,' Sigourney told *New York* magazine in June 1984. 'She's not an innocent little fly caught in the spider's web. She's a little spider herself.' As a way of expressing her gender's antagonism towards the play Sigourney wrote a parody entitled *Hurlygirly* which the cast actually performed during the play's pre-Broadway run at the Goodman Theatre in Chicago. Once in New York *Hurlyburly* quickly established itself among theatre-goers as the play to see. Reviews were excellent; both the production and the script were highly commended. 'It is an important work, masterfully accomplished' – *Time*. But it was the actors who received the most acclaim. 'They are all superb,' raved *Newsweek*. In a play so uniquely strong in ensemble-acting the task of picking out the best individual actor or performance was an impossibility. Yet when the 1984 Broadway Tony Award nominations were released Sigourney found herself amongst those vying for Best Actress. Her performance had been exemplary, despite the fact that she radiates too much intelligence and poise on stage to warrant playing a bimbo. But the nomination suggested that at last her peers were beginning to acknowledge her as an accomplished stage actress.

Midway through the triumphant run of *Hurlyburly*, Sigourney announced that she would be leaving the production in October. She had fallen in love with a man six years her junior, Jim Simpson, a theatre director, born and raised in Hawaii, and they planned to marry in the fall. The roots of their relationship go back to the early eighties when the two of them used to attend the summer theatre festivals at Williamstown, Massachusetts regularly. Sigourney was acquainted with the talented and upwardly mobile Jim Simpson, but their paths scarcely crossed. On the odd occasion they bumped into each other and indulged in innocent conversation, but nothing more. This went on until the summer of 1983, when Sigourney appeared in Harold Pinter's *Old Times*. At last they found themselves involved in the same production. He was in charge of the non-Equity players. Working with him on a day-to-day basis Sigourney found herself growing quite fond of the young man. One night at a party Weaver went over to Jim and asked him for the next dance, a request that was refused. 'Luckily, we had another chance,' said Sigourney. Destiny is difficult to shake off or escape. It does seem that they were fated to meet and be together: their lives had been running parallel courses, and there are some striking similarities in their backgrounds. For example, both had grown up in a show business environment, although the circumstances were different. Jim Simpson had been a child actor appearing in a succession of television shows and movies. He later regularly worked on one of the most popular TV cop shows of all time, *Hawaii Five-O*. While many of us would have been gladly content with such a life style, Jim hungered for other challenges. Most importantly of all he wanted to achieve a higher standard of education. So he swapped the idyllic Hawaiian world of palm trees and soft, warm breezes for Boston, where he attended the city's university for four years. Like Sigourney he was a top student and went on to enrol at the Yale School of Drama. Jim's stay at the academy was certainly less traumatic than his soul-mate's. He enjoyed the courses and was spurred on by his teachers. At an important crossroad in his life Simpson decided to abandon acting and instead channel his considerable talents into theatre directing. His first real professional theatrical duties were at Williamstown in the early eighties. He also worked at one of Sigourney's old haunts, Joseph Papp's Public Theatre.

In October 1983 Sigourney was preparing a guest list for a Halloween party she was holding in her apartment (an appropriate theme given the nature of her role in *Ghostbusters*), when she remembered the gifted director and invited him to come along. At first Jim Simpson, a shy and very private person like Sigourney, wasn't keen on the idea, but he agreed to attend after being seduced by the persuasive charms of some of Sigourney's friends. Amidst all the noise and excitement of the party Sigourney finally managed to corner him alone. Together they sat and talked for much of the night. Both were silently but consciously captivated by one another: she by his talent and wealth of knowledge about the theatre; and he by her extraordinary beauty, wit and intelligence. Most of all, he was impressed by her powerful personality. This was no ordinary actress – or woman, for that matter – she was a true original, deeply committed to her craft. She was in the business because she loved the theatre, the very process of acting, and not for mere fame and fortune. By the end of the party Sigourney, taking the lead once again, invited him around for a quiet dinner for two the following evening. From those first two tentative nights there developed a serious and passionate romance. Both were surprised to discover just how close they felt and how much they had in common. The fact that each of them had graduated from Yale led to many hours reminiscing about past teachers and classes. Their fascination for all aspects of the theatre also drew them deeper into love. Soon they were seen everywhere together, always engrossed in conversation, always enjoying one another's company. When Sigourney took Jim home to meet her parents she sneakily introduced him as a surfer, mindful of the fact that her father would approve more of a surfer dating his daughter than some theatre type. Despite working in the same world and sharing similar interests the couple were able to open new doors for each other. Most importantly for Sigourney Jim kept her in touch with what was happening on the theatre scene at a time when she was becoming more and more immersed in movies. 'He brought me back into a world I might have been stepping out of now.'

The couple enjoyed twelve long, happy months of courtship, which included camping (one of Sigourney's favourite pursuits), in Simpson's native Hawaii. The seriousness of the affair was apparent when the normally hyper-secretive Sigourney, cryptic and elusive about personal matters, began to open the floodgates of her heart to journalists. There was a time when the actress would either blankly refuse to discuss her love life in interview situations or sit back and gamely spoof it. (Sigourney had once told a gullible journalist that she and old love James McClure had been married for fifteen years and had five illegitimate children.) But now she seemed almost anxious to talk about her feelings for Simpson. At first there were subtle hints, veiled suggestions that she was falling madly in love, but these soon gave way to more openness and honesty about their relationship. Although Sigourney remained adamant that marriage was out of the question, in fact it was just a year away.

When Sigourney Weaver married Jim Simpson in mid-October 1984 the wildly unorthodox and irregular ceremony beautifully complemented the freakish and eccentric nature of the couple. Jim was another free spirit. 'I mean, we're talking about someone who didn't wear shoes until he was ten.' The ceremony was held on the hallowed turf of her father's Long Island yacht club, a traditional setting for what was the most untraditional wedding of the year. The musical accompaniment to the service was provided by bongo drums and bagpipes and two ministers, one male, the other female, were asked to perform the ceremony jointly. The most bizarre touch of all was that everyone was given a wash-off tattoo to wear. This wasn't compulsory but most of the guests, including Bill Murray, entered into the spirit of the proceedings. 'It was great fun,' recalled the comedian. 'But then I've never seen Sigourney give a bad party.' The other more stiff and conservative guests must have questioned whether this was really the best way to conduct a serious wedding ceremony. But those who knew how unconventional Sigourney and Jim could be had a great time and decided these were all healthy signs of a good, fun marriage: they made the perfect couple. Sigourney's mother was one of those who were a little bemused by the strange goings-on. 'Our wedding was sort of crazy', Sigourney told *Première* magazine in 1988. 'I know my mother is a little upset that she didn't get more of a hand in the wedding. But it was utterly our wedding and, in that sense, a celebration.' Nevertheless, the Weavers were overjoyed at their daughter's obvious happiness. They were glad, and a little relieved, that she had finally settled down into marriage: at thirty-five it was about time. Surprisingly, given Sigourney's independent nature, married life suited her admirably. She was on the threshold of a great adventure, and needed little encouragement from reporters to give progress reports. Jim Simpson had arrived at precisely the right time in Sigourney's life. She had now reached the point in her career where she was an established film personality and actor. Marriage happened at the exact juncture at which Sigourney discovered that she wanted more from life than simply to make movies.

Just after Sigourney had finished making *Alien* (which in her own words 'had been an awful experience'), she visited a clairvoyant in London. The actress decided not to reveal her connections with show business and even told the psychic that her name was Susan. But the woman was able to grasp everything. She sensed that Sigourney was in the public eye and worked with exciting people. The clairvoyant made numerous reassuring comments which helped her enormously, and even singled out a few important events in her life, past and future. But when she looked at Sigourney's palm the woman gave a gasp. 'You were in a bad place; it's not good. It's in the past.' Sigourney figured it had to be the Yale Drama School. Most interesting of all, the clairvoyant told Sigourney that she wouldn't marry until she was thirty-five. 'I sort of screamed,' she described to *Interview* magazine in July 1988. 'It was eight years away. I thought, God, it's a lifetime.' Sigourney married Jim Simpson a week before she turned thirty-five. Fate indeed.

Although husband and wife were both in the entertainment business, by no stretch of the imagination could Jim be classed in the same league as Sigourney. He was a respected director in theatrical circles but a complete unknown in the eyes of the public. Sigourney was now a major star thanks to the success of *Ghostbusters*. Her being the celebrity, the centre of attention and the object of much public adulation, could have had an adverse effect on the marriage. Luckily over the years the couple have managed to remain relatively untouched by Sigourney's elevated public status. Living in New York they both feel fairly aloof from the whole showbiz thing. Sigourney herself tends not to think too much about fame, although she is aware of being recognized wherever she goes, 'which is nice and sometimes surprising'. However, gone are the days in the early eighties when she could travel freely on public transport. Today she feels that her freedom has been dramatically restricted by her public status. She can no longer ride on the subways as frequently as she would like, 'and I often have to walk around looking at the sidewalk'.

Deep within Sigourney there lingers a genuine fear of being confronted by a fan or an anonymous person in a crowded street. Luckily such occurrences only happen periodically. All the glittering advantages and trappings of fame can at times count for very little. The chances of a star enjoying a life of seclusion and privacy, relatively free from prying eyes and the unscrupulous tabloid press, are remote indeed. Members of the public seem to expect celebrities to behave like their screen personas in real life. 'You have to be charming to strangers who grow angry and scream at you because they feel you owe them more than a screen performance.' Sigourney, in particular, finds such restrictions uncomfortable to say the least. Whilst in the public domain, shopping or seeing a play, she rarely signs autographs. Selfish or not Sigourney has grown jaded of being forced to run down streets or jump into hired cars in order to avoid crazed fans. 'I'm afraid to leave the theatre without a friend. It's like running the gauntlet.' But living in New York has given Sigourney a valuable shield of anonymity. Native New Yorkers are renowned for their general nonchalance around stars: they don't really care and tend to leave them alone.

9 *Scraping the Barrel*

Marriage, far from settling Sigourney Weaver, sparked off the most productive phase of her career to date. During the course of 1985 the actress made three films in quick succession. Only the blockbusting *Aliens* turned out to be of any merit: the other two films were the worst of her career – *Half Moon Street*, a turgid thriller; and *A Woman or Two*, a French comedy that simply wasn't funny. This represented a missed opportunity: the characters she played in these films were amongst the toughest and most fascinating of her career.

A Woman or Two features a charismatic central performance from French superstar Gerard Depardieu and fine cinematography by Carlo Varini, but little else. Depardieu plays Julien, an archaeologist who unearths the 2-million-year-old fossilized remains of the first Frenchwoman in the Dordogne. His discovery attracts the attention of an American foundation who agree to finance all further research. When Julien is dispatched to meet the institute's representative at the airport he mistakenly introduces himself to advertising executive Jessica Fitzgerald (Sigourney Weaver, in the most mediocre performance of her career). The ambitious Jessica hits upon the notion of using the skeleton to promote a new brand of perfume. Achingly unfunny antics ensue, culminating in the startling revelation that the first Frenchwoman was black.

The role of Jessica presented Sigourney with possibly the most difficult challenge of her career. The picture was to be made in Paris with a continental film crew. Director Daniel Vigne asked his star if she felt competent enough to perform in French. Sigourney responded positively, if a little cautiously. 'My French was articulate, but not the easy, bright, idiomatic French of the character,' she disclosed to *Elle* magazine in October 1986. 'But if I put my mind to something ... ' This is the kind of bravado that fits in nicely with the character of Jessica, whose pursuit of any chosen course of action with blinkered determination is a trait that Sigourney shares. Working in Europe and making a film away from the rules and influence of Hollywood was a dramatic and refreshing change. Few major American stars successfully make the transition to the continental style of film-making and people like Robert De Niro and Burt Lancaster who appear in foreign productions tend to have their lines dubbed. But Sigourney insisted that her own voice was to be used and charged into an exhaustive five week, eight hours a day, refresher course in French. She endured three additional weeks under the direction of a private coach to sharpen her control of the language further. Then Vigne threatened to dishonour her with a contractual clause stating that the actress could be dubbed if she failed to achieve a certain standard. Sigourney reacted violently to the proposal. 'No way,' she screamed. 'Not after the work I've done.' By the end of filming Sigourney was in such a confident mood that she was even improvising in French.

Sigourney's stay in Paris was tinged with sadness. The newlyweds had spent a comparatively short time together before she had to dash off to France to begin work on *A Woman or Two*. Due to work commitments Jim was forced to stay behind in America. Sigourney desperately missed him; it pained her that they had to be parted so soon after the marriage. But the couple were aware that they would often be separated because of the special demands of their work (a state of affairs that Sigourney scarcely relished). She shivered at the mere thought of being away too long from her husband. This sense of attachment was something new in this powerfully liberated and independent lady. She came relatively late to marriage, and even then it had to take fourth place after *A Woman or Two, Half Moon Street*, and *Aliens*. Only then could she give total commitment to her marriage. To be fair it wasn't Sigourney's intention to spend so much time abroad filming so soon after her marriage vows. But being presented with three great roles in one year was an offer she just couldn't afford to turn down. For an actress

Sigourney and her husband, theatre director Jim Simpson. The couple married in 1984.

Sigourney, sporting a severe hair cut, arrives at Heathrow Airport with husband Jim Simpson and baby daughter Charlotte to begin work on *Alien III* (1992).

Sigourney and her beloved New York.

such opportunities are rare indeed. Sigourney called it 'a miracle'. Jim Simpson has always appreciated the actor's psyche, and was most understanding about his wife's position. This is one of the advantages of marrying a fellow-artist, someone who is comfortable with, and well-adapted to, living within the competitive and fast world of entertainment. Another person might take great exception to his brand-new wife flying off to Europe to work. Jim, however, was very supportive. 'Any success I've had so far juggling my private and professional lives is because of Jim's generosity,' she told *Film Comment* in 1986. 'He's made more compromises than I have without billing me for it.' One such compromise was that he was prepared to give up work for several months to lend moral support to his wife while she was making *Aliens* in London. He was charitable and encouraging when Sigourney didn't have much time or energy for their marriage. Sigourney feels that the fact that Jim is younger has helped the marriage enormously. 'It's wonderful to live with someone who believes you can do anything – especially for a woman. It's so supportive, and so rare,' she told *Film Comment* in December 1986. (However, when some of her friends suggested she go into politics, Simpson was quick to draw the line.) Without her husband's backing Sigourney is adamant that she would never have been able to tackle all three films. *Aliens* would have been the casualty simply because it was the last offer. 'You can film only for so long without a home life or else you go batty. And I had this wonderful home life'.

Being alone in Paris, the most romantic city in the world, made Sigourney miss Jim even more. But she managed as best she could and spent many happy hours finding her way around and adapting to the Parisian way of life. She also became quite friendly with the French film crew, who adored her, and got on particularly well with her co-star. Lovers on screen, Sigourney and Depardieu enjoyed a healthy working relationship. She fondly remembers his practical jokes and adolescent sense of humour, which kept her and the crew in perennial high spirits throughout filming. 'He was great. We had a wonderful time together. He's certainly the most mischievous actor I've ever worked with, which I adore because I like that.' Sigourney left the picture with respect for him as an actor and a Frenchman, and hoped that one day they might have the chance to collaborate on a more serious film. She would have made a perfect foil for him in *Green Card*, his first English language feature. In *A Woman or Two* their inspired pairing failed to produce any on-screen fireworks.

With the odd notable exception, subtitled movies tend to be frowned upon in America: they are seen as too highbrow for the average cinemagoer, and are often relegated to the sparsely attended art house circuit. Despite the 'name' presence of Sigourney Weaver, *A Woman or Two* was subjected to a very limited release in February 1987. Not surprisingly, it sunk without a trace and was uniformly slated. Critics found the film muddled, clumsy and unfunny. Sigourney didn't escape from the débâcle unscathed. 'Weaver, speaking an accurate but toneless school room French, has little of the natural eccentricity that great beauties need to play comedy. She is stiff and severe.' – *New York*. *The Village Voice* was similarly unimpressed, calling her performance 'one long void'. Served by a particularly feeble script Sigourney looks distinctly uncomfortable in almost every scene in which she appears. She tackles the accent with a great deal of bravery and competence, but she can't overcome the difficulties of playing comedy in another language. Most of her energy is spent worrying about pronouncing her *r*'s and *eu*'s correctly, which does create tensions that leave her performance stilted, strained, and unrealistic. This was not a happy piece of casting. For Sigourney the shooting of *A Woman or Two* was problematic. There were great differences between Vigne and herself about how comedy should be played. She felt that the film's style vacillated awkwardly between realism and farce, a viewpoint shared by Depardieu. One moment the film is an opera bouffe comedy; then it's slapstick; then 1930s American screwball, with particular allusion to *Bringing up Baby*; and finally a bit of sex comedy is thrown in for good measure – all of which fail to gel satisfactorily. Sigourney is well known for wanting to make changes to scripts if she feels that her part is ill-defined in certain areas or that dialogue is poor. 'I've always been outspoken. I think it's a service to the writer. Having written my own stuff, I know it's important to get feedback.' She believes that she is hired in part because she has the capacity to be objective and to say what she thinks about a scene. She's not particularly concerned about always getting her own way; she just cares about being heard. One can gauge Sigourney Weaver's antipathy towards Vigne's movie by her contemptuous reference to it as 'that French film'. Once again her much vaunted ambition to play comedy had backfired.

From Paris and the miserable ineptness of *A Woman or Two*, Sigourney flew to London to begin work on a film that turned out to be just as much of a disaster. *Half Moon Street* teamed Sigourney up with one of cinema's most enduring stars, Michael Caine. The film was based on the novella *Dr Slaughter* by Paul Theroux (published under the title *Half Moon Street* in America), a complex and highly erotic, some would say sordid, piece of literature. Sigourney plays Lauren Slaughter, a Harvard Ph.D., who works in the London Institute for Middle Eastern Affairs. To supplement her meagre income she joins an exclusive escort agency and becomes a high-class call-girl. Through her dubious moonlighting activities she meets Lord Bulbeck (Caine), a top-ranking politician engaged in delicate negotiations for an Arab–Israeli peace settlement. As the two lovers grow ever closer, Lauren Slaughter is inextricably drawn into Bulbeck's dangerous world and unknowingly becomes involved in a seedy terrorist plot to assassinate him.

The men responsible for bringing Theroux's story to the screen were British producer Geoffrey Reeve and Bob Swaim, the American director of the police thriller *La Balance*, which won the French equivalent of an Oscar. Since then offers from Hollywood had poured in, including the chance to direct *Beverly Hills Cop*. But Swaim turned such commercial fare down in preference for more unusual and original material. After the hard-boiled machismo of *La Balance*, Swaim expressed a desire to make a 'feminine' picture, a portrait of a strong and self-confident woman of the eighties. *Half Moon Street* seemed the perfect vehicle. At the same time, he could comment on the state of London in the 1980s, a city which he believed had become a much more violent place to live. In the film we see car bombs exploding in broad daylight; evidence of corruption in high places; an abundance of Arab terrorists in Mayfair. Although Swaim's cosmopolitan, multi-cultural vision of London is a little unrealistic, it is an interesting outsider's view of this great city.

Swaim's major problem was the casting of the female protagonist. Many of the actresses who read for the part were put off by the sleazy material and the nudity involved. Sigourney, however, fell under the spell of Lauren Slaughter. Quite simply it was the best part Sigourney had ever read and she fought hard to win the role. Slaughter was totally original, a dynamic part, and a marked contrast to the one-dimensional women inhabiting the majority of scripts that fell through her mail-box. Here was the perfect opportunity to move away from the sophisticate she had personified in recent films, and get to grips with new and exciting characterization. Portraying a prostitute would be a welcome change and prove to producers that she was capable of perceptibly widening her range. (Again we see Sigourney's fondness for challenges and her eagerness to play against type.) Prior to her involvement on *Half Moon Street*, Sigourney was unfamiliar with the work of Paul Theroux, although she did subsequently read the author's best-known novel *The Mosquito Coast*, and boasts of being the person who suggested to Peter Weir that it should be filmed. Weir took her advice and the movie emerged in 1986 with the compelling Harrison Ford (a future Weaver co-star) in the lead. Sigourney adored the *Dr Slaughter* book. 'It's one blow job after another,' she told *Film Comment* in December 1986. 'I adored it because it's a real satire. My father-in-law read it, then my father, then my mother-in-law, who had the good taste not to mention it to me.' But she had little fondness for the way Theroux actually depicted Slaughter. In the book she is a very unsympathetic character, an egoist, very closed, and she deals out her sex coldly. There's very little pleasure in her pleasure. Sigourney argued: 'My role is immensely improved by me.'

Slaughter is an intelligent and beautiful woman, brimming over with self-confidence. She is also a practical individual; her decision to sell her body is motivated by a pragmatic need to make money, and a craving to satisfy what appears to be an insatiable sexual appetite. She returns from a depressing three-year field trip to China looking for a good time; she wants fun and as many bed companions as she can muster. The film implies that women get just as much of a kick from casual sex as men. In one scene Lauren Slaughter confesses to Bulbeck that 'a lot of women like uncomplicated sex'. This was Sigourney's own line; she put it into the script. This viewpoint drew a heated response from groups of feminists who complained that the film was yet another to perpetuate the male fantasy of women as available sex objects. Slaughter has a refreshingly open and relaxed attitude towards sex. She challenges hypocritical attitudes by embarking upon a way of life that labels her a slut. A man doing a similar thing would be considered a playboy. She is not ashamed of what she does. In marked contrast to the other escort girls represented in the film, who hide behind masks of their own creation and are totally impersonal, Lauren uses her own name and is herself on her dates. In this way she doesn't feel like a victim. She has the illusion of power over men, however. Although she is being abused she naïvely believes that she remains in control of the situation. Only towards the end does she realize that she has been exploited all along. 'She's been stupid. Her arrogance is a character flaw. Any tragedy that comes out of a character flaw interests me,' Sigourney told *Film Comment* in December 1986.

Due to the risqué source material Swaim found a swell of resistance building up against his picture. One Hollywood executive dismissed Theroux's book as 'unfilmable pornography'. Not surprisingly, financial backing was difficult to obtain; studios queued up to turn the project down. After several re-writes of the script RKO became interested and were responsible for gathering further American money to cover the $8m budget. Sigourney arrived in London shortly before filming began on 5 August 1985. She was happy to be back in Britain again and making another film in London, her first since *Alien* six years before. (Sigourney would stay on in the capital to make *Aliens*, residing in an attractive flat in the trendier reaches of Chelsea.) After half a year in London the idea of living in the city on a more permanent basis appealed to her enormously. Sigourney has a great love and fondness for the UK. 'Every time I visit I feel at home there. I love being English.' She adores the English countryside, particularly the Lake District and the Cotswolds, and many of her relatives live in Hampshire, Dorset, and Oxford. Whilst in London Sigourney made a special point of visiting Langan's Brasserie in Piccadilly, a fine establishment partly owned by her co-star in *Half Moon Street*, Michael Caine.

During filming Swaim was under considerable pressure to tone down the sexual aspect of the story. When Sigourney read the revised screenplay she was angry and disappointed at how tame the whole thing had become. On location the actress was a lone voice pleading with Swaim not to make *Half Moon Street* as a 'safe' picture. In her opinion the director had lost creative control of the production and failed to fight for the original concept. 'He changed my character into this humourless looker with brains that had nothing to do with my idea of the character nor Paul Theroux's novel,' Sigourney confessed to *Time Out* in January 1989. Artistically the only consolation lay in the experience of working with Caine, whose approach to acting was completely different from her own. Before taking on a role Sigourney likes to carry out extensive research into the background of the character, to explore all the facets of the woman she intends to play. Caine ignores such weighty 'method' preparation; he just worries about his lines and when and where he's supposed to say them. Once, during the execution of a particulary difficult scene Caine remarked, 'I'm going to do this in one take so I can get home to dinner and see my wife.' Sigourney had never encountered anyone like him. Instead of being repelled by such behaviour Sigourney found Michael Caine's relaxed way of working, and his whole perspective on the business, very refreshing. He was such a consummate professional and had so much experience that acting now came to him intuitively. Sigourney still broke down her scripts and figured them out as she would a play. In many respects she continued to approach cinema as if it were the theatre. *Half Moon Street* was a dispiriting ordeal, apart from the joy of acting with Caine. They have remained good friends ever since. But their relationship had unfortunate beginnings: due to poor planning the first scene they shot together was their big love scene. The two actors had barely met, but what could have been a difficult and embarrassing day of filming was made bearable by Caine's considerable charm and good humour.

Although Sigourney had never appeared naked on film before, the prospect of removing her clothes in front of a movie camera didn't really bother her that much. She is often asked to participate in gratuitous nude scenes. (She appeared partially undressed in *A Woman or Two*.) Before both of these films Sigourney, an acknowledged beauty and sex symbol, had splendidly demonstrated the art of being able to inject sex into a scene without discarding a scrap of clothing. Her famous siren role in *Ghostbusters* is a prime example of this. We are privy to only a few suggestive shots of her long, sleek legs and nothing more, yet she brilliantly communicates to the audience a sense of mounting sexual energy, sending pulses racing across the nation. For Sigourney the decision to play a nude scene is just as important as the decision to appear in a scene of violence. There is nothing the least prim or prudish about Sigourney Weaver; she has no objection to nudity in film *per se*, as long as she feels that it is an important element of the film and not exploitative. For instance, Sigourney managed to persuade Daniel Vigne to make severe cuts to the love scene in *A Woman or Two* because she felt there was too much emphasis on her nude form. In Weaver's opinion the scenes of nakedness in *Half Moon Street* were perfectly justifiable and were not a crude attempt to garner publicity and draw people to the cinema. Yet one is left to ponder on the reason why Sigourney allowed herself to be talked into doing such pointless and cheaply voyeuristic scenes as those in *Half Moon Street*. She appears topless in a bath, on an exercise bike and in stockings and suspenders with her bare buttocks to the camera. Sigourney's long-awaited 'bare all' scenes are tacky in the extreme, exploitative, and very unflattering. They are nowhere near as effective as, nor have the erotic power of, Kathleen Turner's sensational strip in *Body Heat* for example. If a Hollywood actress is going to make the difficult decision to appear naked then she might as well do so in some style. Swaim is to blame here: he directs the random sex scenes in a very emotionless fashion. Sigourney was attacked in some quarters for appearing nude in such a futile and shabby way. The *Evening Standard* was the harshest: 'The discreetly sexy Ms Weaver abandons her clothes along with her judgement in this worthless pile of junk, thereby shattering the illusion that she (a) is an intelligent actress and (b) has a great body.'

Half Moon Street opened in America on 26 September 1986 in a re-edited and re-scored form due to a string of unenthusiastic preview screenings. The movie, a box-office disaster, was slain by the critics. *Variety* described it as 'a half-baked excuse for a film'. In spite of the script's implausibilities and ineptness Sigourney gives a commendable performance. She dominates *Half Moon Street* as she had none of her previous films up to that time, save *Alien*. (William Hurt occupied most of the screen time in *The Janitor*; Linda Hunt walked effortlessly away with the acting honours in *The Year of Living Dangerously*; and the special effects in *Ghostbusters* eclipsed all the human performers.) Unfortunately, Swaim's movie isn't on a par with Sigourney's acting. This is a shame because Lauren Slaughter is one of the most fascinating and complex roles Sigourney has played. From such original and bizarre material Swaim had managed to make a feeble and pedestrian motion picture. Roll on *Aliens*.

10 *This Time It's War*

In the seven years since its release *Alien* had achieved a degree of cult status among fantasy purists, many saw Scott's work as the quintessential sci-fi-horror movie, a stylish, spine-chilling thriller that spawned a mini plague of cheap spin-offs but amazingly defied legitimate attempts to generate a worthy sequel.

The rights to an *Alien* follow-up were jointly owned by the original co-producers, Walter Hill, Gordon Carroll, and David Giler. Sigourney had remained on friendly terms with all three men and occasionally the group would get together over dinner and entertain thoughts about a sequel. One humorous continuation idea had a salvage crew picking up Ripley's escape craft. They open up her sleeping pod and she dissolves into dust, thus paving the way for an all-new set of characters. This and other submitted screenplays and concepts failed to gain the interest of the producers so, in 1984, the planned *Alien* sequel was temporarily scrapped in preference for a fresh project, a science fiction version of *Spartacus*. James Cameron, the young director of the cult fantasy hit *The Terminator*, was invited to help on the script. Like so many of today's top directors (Coppola, Scorsese), Cameron was a protégé of the Roger Corman Film School where he worked on such low-grade epics as *Battle Beyond the Stars* and *Escape from New York*. He made his directorial début with the worthless *Piranha II* in 1981 and also co-wrote *Rambo: First Blood Part II* with Sylvester Stallone. Cameron did not share Hill and Giler's passion for a *Spartacus* remake. What he really wanted to do was direct the follow-up to *Alien*, which was one of his favourite movies. After he submitted a forty-five page treatment based on a screenplay called *Mother*, the story of which concerned an alien queen, which he had written soon after seeing *Alien*, the producers gave Cameron the green light.

Cameron immediately set to work on a screenplay, carefully plotting the entire emphasis of the story around the character of Ripley, even though Sigourney had not been contacted. (The actress was not contractually obliged to return.) After working solidly on the script for three and a half months Cameron was annoyed when he discovered that she had still not been informed about his project. In the end he telephoned Sigourney himself, but she wasn't exactly keen on the idea of doing a sequel and was deeply sceptical of the whole thing. She thought Cameron only wanted her in a scene-setting role and that Ripley would then be killed off. Sigourney also feared that a sequel, despite arriving some six years after the original and therefore not a blatant rip-off, would still be seeking to profit by the success of the *Alien* formula perfected by Ridley Scott. She had no intention of becoming involved in a film that was produced purely to make money for 20th Century Fox. She wanted to know why Cameron wished to make the sequel and if his intentions were honourable. Despite her strong early misgivings a meeting between the two was arranged. Sigourney found Cameron a genuinely talented and dedicated craftsman and recognized within him a sincere love of and commitment to the project. She also admired the way in which he wanted the *Alien* saga to progress and develop. This was a man who would be worth working with. Most of all, she was impressed by the way Cameron had treated Ripley. On reading the script Sigourney was surprised to find that her character dominated the narrative; Ripley was in virtually every scene. This was in marked contrast to the first film, where she had been pretty one-dimensional, only emerging as the primary character towards the end. Scott had deliberately de-emphasized Ripley in order to keep the audience guessing who would survive. But Cameron wanted the focus on Ripley right from the start, a factor that had some bearing on Weaver's decision to return. (She would also receive a fee of $1 million for her services – nearly thirty times more than her 1979 salary!) Sigourney also knew that Cameron wasn't willing to make the sequel without her. 'I was egotistical enough to be moved by that.'

Cameron's film takes place fifty-seven years on from the original. Still in the grip of hypersleep Ripley's escape ship is picked up by a space station orbiting the earth. She awakes only to make the horrific discovery that the planet on which the *Nostromo* crew landed has been colonized. Earth's bureaucrats dismiss Ripley's story of an alien encounter until they lose contact with the colonists. Reluctantly Ripley agrees to accompany a crack troop of 21st-century marines on a rescue mission to the barren planet. Ripley is a changed woman in *Aliens*, no longer the eager young space ensign of Scott's film. Those experiences have left her mentally scarred and her life is all but destroyed. Cut off from her own time, yet still haunted by the past, Ripley is alone, family and friends are long dead. Here Ripley is seen as a social outcast, distrusted by all. She has almost become an alien herself. Sigourney found Ripley's predicament a provocative one and tried to imagine how this would effect her. This was part of the challenge of playing the character again: she was almost a completely different woman. But the attributes that Sigourney had so admired in the old Ripley still shine through: her leadership qualities and gritty determination. Despite finding herself in the future Ripley's grasp of advanced technology is outstanding; she operates every machine and space age weapon with ease, and out-thinks and out-fights every man in the combat team.

Once on the planet Ripley's team finds a young girl, Newt, the sole survivor of the Acheron colony. Cameron's original intention was to begin the film with a long sequence showing us how the alien horde invaded the colony. Newt's parents come across the derelict ship from the first film, and Newt's father is attacked and impregnated by an alien. One assumes that the colonists all suffer the same hideous fate which befell the crew of the *Nostromo*. These missing fifteen minutes were to have been inserted back into the movie on a 'special edition' video in 1990, but it never materialized. The friendship between Ripley and Newt is at the core of the film and Ripley's maternal instinct is Cameron's strongest theme. In another important scene omitted from the final print Ripley is told that her daughter has grown old and died while she was lost in space. Sigourney used a picture of her own mother to react to when Ripley is shown a photograph of her silver-haired daughter. The loss of Ripley's daughter explains why she is so attached to Newt. This was the aspect of the story that appealed to Sigourney the most. 'And I got terribly upset when it was cut out,' she explained to *Première* magazine in October 1988, 'That's the whole reason I did the movie.' But Cameron felt the idea was just too perfect: Ripley loses her daughter then finds a substitute in the guise of Newt. In his opinion there were other less predictable bonding elements between the two. Newt has also come face to face with the alien, she knows what it is capable of and, most importantly, she is also lost and alone. Cameron felt that the extra concept of Newt filling the gap of Ripley's dead daughter wasn't needed. This was the only difference of opinion between Weaver and Cameron about the interpretation of the character. On the whole they both worked supremely well together. By the end of filming Cameron had nothing but respect for the actress.

The theme of motherhood permeates the entire work, from Ripley's to the alien queen furiously protecting her offspring. The film makes it clear that the queen is not inherently evil, she's only doing what Ripley is trying to do: to survive and to protect children. 'Everybody may think we're making a monster film, but we're really making a film about motherhood,' Sigourney told reporters. The climax is a post-feminist slugging match between Ripley (dressed in a kind of combat suit), and the mother alien, for custody of Newt. It is a truly astonishing scene. This is what Cameron has been leading up to, a fight to the death between the two female protagonists.

Aliens is also about heroism and courage, about being pushed to the very limit of endurance and then finding the resources to carry on. This theme is crystallized in the sequence where Ripley risks her life to rescue Newt from the clutches of an alien spawn. Cameron was fascinated by the plight of Ripley. How does someone who has gone through a personal hell put the pieces of their lives back together again, and how do they react if they are faced with such horrors again? Would they collapse under the pressure or emerge stronger? Ripley must return to that dead planet of nightmares and confront her demons. The trip back to Acheron is a kind of exorcism. In *Aliens* all the female characters are stronger than the men. In the end it is Ripley and Newt, the real survivors, who are of heroic mould and who make the final stand. The bullish marines are the first to crack up. Even the queen is more interesting because of her maternal strength. 'And who's interested in fighting a dumb monster?' said Sigourney. Working with Carrie Henn, the child actress who portrayed Newt, gave Sigourney various insights into her future role as a mother. 'You don't nurture and protect children,' she told *Film Comment* in December 1986. 'You just talk and are equals. Any attempt on my part to guide or instruct was met with amusement by her.'

By the time *Aliens* began filming on 30 September 1985 Sigourney had been working non-stop in Europe. She was exhausted. She had only finished her role on *Half Moon Street* a few days before she was needed on the *Aliens* set. Despite fears that she would be too tired Sigourney managed to find a reserve of energy and by the third day she was in top gear. Amongst the cast of relative newcomers like Michael Biehn and Paul Reiser, Sigourney was the veteran, the star. The actors and the crew all looked to her for guidance and inspiration. For the first time a major movie rested on her broad shoulders. She revelled in the responsibility of carrying the *Alien* sequel, of having the leading role. Almost every day she would be on the set, looking over the script, sorting out problems. The crew were crazy about her. Such dedication, far from tiring the actress out, was just the tonic she needed. At intervals the rest of the cast would go off on mini-breaks into London or over to Paris, but Sigourney was never once envious of her fellow actors' freedom: she enjoyed going into work everyday, she felt like the film's anchor, always there if anyone needed her.

The four months of live action photography took place at Pinewood under a cloak of secrecy. All of the sets were closed to visitors (some scenes were shot at a disused power station in Acton, west London), plot details were kept away from journalists, and only the official stills photographer had the authority to take pictures. The production team bristled with some of the finest and most experienced effects people in the business, including John Richardson, noted for his work on *Superman* and the James Bond movies, and Brian Johnson who won an Oscar for *The Empire Strikes Back*. Johnson had also worked on *Alien*, but other veterans from the 1979 film were a rare sight. This was a deliberate move on the part of Cameron so that his picture would not consciously follow the visual splendour evoked by Scott. (Incidentally, the two directors did meet up at Pinewood, where Scott was filming *Legend*. He would later call *Aliens* a 'worthy successor'.) Another notable absentee, H.R. Giger, was contacted but he was busy working on the sequel to *Poltergeist*. Instead Stan Winston, who was responsible for the robotic effects on *The Terminator*, created the creatures.

One of the main visual features of *Aliens* is the hardware, particularly the weaponry. The marines are equipped with enough guns and ammunition to wipe out a small army. Weaver had watched *The Terminator* shortly before meeting Cameron for the first time and surprised herself by enjoying it immensely. However, she never expected there to be so much militarism in *Aliens*. Sigourney had been so busy reading the script for human values that she had inadvertently skipped over all the references to guns. Only later did she admit that she had totally underestimated the film's reliance on violence and weapons. To her it was much more interesting to try and outwit the alien than blindly shoot the poor thing down. Almost daily the cast were subjected to gun and grenade practice. For an actress who is involved in a gun-control lobby in America it was an embarrassing dilemma to be acting in a film which promoted the use of weapons to such a high degree. The irony was not lost on Sigourney Weaver. Yet her experiences did serve a moral purpose. Handling those destructive weapons gave Sigourney a tremendous sensation of power, making her realize just how dangerous they can be. 'They intoxicate because they make you feel so powerful,' Sigourney said to the *Daily Express* in August 1986. 'Now I'm more against them than I was when I started the film.' She also blamed Ripley's reliance on nicotine as the reason for her renewed dependence on cigarettes. Sigourney never smokes at home because of the smell. She dislikes the stench of smoke on her fingers and on her hair and clothes. But on the *Aliens* set smoking was a way of taking a quick break, a moment of inner relaxation amidst all the pressure. Smoking was one of two bad habits that Sigourney picked up in Britain. The other was a craving for take-away hamburgers at those rather dubious street vendors that she wouldn't go near back home in New York.

One of the main criticisms levelled against the film was its simplistic militarist mentality. If *Alien* was a fifties B-movie shocker set in space, then the sequel was a science fiction version of a war film. In *Aliens* Cameron sought to lampoon the world of Rambo and his ilk, but his images of war are laden with graphic realism and are chillingly reminiscent of Vietnam. The marines are a *Dirty Dozen*-type bunch; their 'Let's nuke 'em' attitude and the film's confrontational politics caused consternation amongst some critics. Sigourney managed a brave face. 'Just call me Rambolina,' she joked. But behind the smile lay a genuine fear. The tabloids had hailed her as cinema's toughest new champion and gloated over the fact that a woman was out-muscling Schwarzenegger and Stallone at the box-office. 'People now say to me "You out-Rambo Rambo." I just shiver down to my shoes.' In fact, Sigourney didn't base her character on the recent batch of tough-guy heroes, but on the women warriors of classic Chinese literature and on the Valkyrie. Cameron also reacted strongly to the accusation that his film was just '*Rambo* in outer space'. He admitted that the films were comparable in action and mayhem, but he felt *Aliens* dealt more with believable people whom the audience comes to care about. Rambo was just a cartoon character, whereas Ripley is an ordinary person: she isn't a trained soldier with robot-like reflexes, she survives through sheer guts and determination. An audience could relate to that. The violence in *Aliens* was also heavily criticized. Sigourney gallantly took most of the blame. 'I did do the movie and I am responsible to a certain extent for the content. I can't defend it,' she told the *Daily Express* in August 1986. However, leading psychiatrists, discussing the film's social implications, praised Weaver's 'kick ass' character for helping the feminist cause. In Ripley women's liberation had found another great fictional heroine.

Although he retained elements of the first film, Cameron's worry that he would be criticized for re-hashing Scott's idea was soon swept aside. *Aliens* is a wholly original piece of film-making. (Stylistically, it owes more to *The Terminator*.) The director skilfully opens out the story; his film is on a much larger scale than Scott's, incorporating more characters and alien creatures. Cameron directs with aplomb and an admirable control of pace. After a slow build-up we are treated to a final hour of heart-stopping action and suspense. A sequel that emerges as a success in its own right is a rare bird. *Aliens* surpasses the original in both entertainment-value and thrills. It is an exceptional movie experience, unquestionably Sigourney's finest work. As Ripley she gives her most compelling performance, completely dominating the film; her aura permeates every frame of celluloid. She manages to make Ripley more sympathetic without sacrificing her toughness. This is star-calibre acting. But thoughts of a return match were quickly silenced by the actress. 'I won't do any more Ripley-like roles. I'm not cutting a career out for myself playing macho women.'

Aliens opened in America on 18 July 1986 and sold $42 million worth of movie tickets. The fifth highest earner of the year, *Aliens* went on to become a worldwide hit, especially in Japan and Britain, and met with a thunderously enthusiastic press response. 'An authentic masterpiece'; 'the scariest movie in the history of cinema'; '*Aliens* is the *Citizen Kane* of science fiction films': these were just some of the mighty accolades Cameron collected. Critics also agreed, unanimously, that Sigourney had created the toughest female screen character ever and that her performance was nothing short of sensational. *Time* magazine called her 'the world's most beautiful, tall, smart woman'. In October 1986 at a gala dinner hosted by America's cinema owners Sigourney was voted Female Star of the Year. This turned out to be the prelude to a far greater honour, her first Oscar nomination. For the first time in cinema history the Academy of Motion Picture Arts and Sciences had nominated a woman appearing in a sci-fi/fantasy film in the category of Best Actress. This was a stunning achievement. One has to go back to 1932 to find the last person to win an Academy Award for a performance in a fantasy movie (and that was a man – Frederic March in *Dr Jekyll and Mr Hyde*). But Sigourney was up against stiff opposition and she didn't fancy her chances. There was Jane Fonda for *The Morning After*, Kathleen Turner for *Peggy Sue Got Married*, Marlee Matlin for *Children of a Lesser God*, and Sissy Spacek for *Crimes of*

Ripley - Sigourney's most famous cinematic creation. Her outstanding performance in *Aliens* (1986) earned her an Oscar nomination.

Sigourney and friend.

Sigourney in a *Vogue* inspired pose.

The role of animal conservationist Dian Fossey in *Gorillas in the Mist* (1988) is the actress's most demanding.

the Heart. Marlee Matlin was the eventual winner.

1985 had been a high-pressure year, but Sigourney still managed to find the time to enjoy her first year of married life. 'Marriage is great fun,' admitted a blissfully contented Sigourney. 'It suits us.' There was even talk about the couple starting a family. 'Jim and I would like to have children,' she told the *Sunday Times* magazine in March 1986. 'And to bring them up ourselves as much as possible. I've waited so long I don't want to miss anything now. It's much more important than career progress.' Although in her late thirties, Sigourney was quick to dismiss suggestions that she was delaying motherhood for too long. The right man had just taken an unusually long time to catch, that was all. Perhaps now was the most propitious time to have children. After the hectic, almost non-stop stretch of work that she had just completed she was ready to settle down and relax for a while, to take a well deserved holiday. 1985 had been an important year of progress and now that was behind her she could get on with living her own life. Although Sigourney would not make another film for a year and a half, work of other kinds still occupied her mind.

A few months after the American release of *Aliens* Sigourney and Jim headed back up to Williamstown for a summer season at a small playhouse, in Tennessee Williams' *Summer and Smoke*. Weaver was paid $400 a week, a far cry from the cool million she had picked up for recreating the role of Ripley. Relatively hefty salaries for movie appearances allows an actress of Sigourney's stature to indulge in smaller and often more artistically worthwhile stage ventures. Returning to her professional homeland after completing a movie is one of the trademarks of Sigourney Weaver's career. 'I find that looking at my career as a revolving door – film, theatre, cabaret, then around again – keeps my enthusiasm high for all those forms,' Sigourney told *Elle* in October 1986. This love of moving between entertainment media has much to do with her liberated nature. Sigourney is always ready to take risks and is constantly open to new and exciting influences. This feeling of invincibility in all aspects of show business is a legacy from those early days when her parents moved house almost on a whim. As a child, Sigourney quickly had to get used to coping and adapting to general changes and different environments. This has helped immeasurably in her acting career.

In addition to her valiant summer-stock voyage, Sigourney began to write again with old favourite Christopher Durang. In this new collaboration she played a character called Sigourney Weaver – 'but I'm a truly horrible creature' – and Durang played a playwright named Christopher Durang. Whoopi Goldberg was also involved, but after her acclaimed performance in Spielberg's *The Colour Purple* had made her an overnight star Sigourney was left wondering if she would want to be involved in their 'stupid little film'. Perhaps the most realistic, and obvious, proposal that came her way in 1986 was the chance to be directed by her husband Jim. The subject of the two of them working together had been raised on more than one occasion in the previous year. The idea sounded hopeful and promised to be fun, but Sigourney disagreed with those who claimed such a union would be a major theatrical event. If such a thing was to happen it was imperative that the couple find the right play. When they did, Sigourney soon discovered that both of them had perhaps bitten off more than they could chew. *The Merchant of Venice* remains William Shakespeare's most controversial work due to its depiction of Shylock, considered by many to be anti-semitic, a gross caricature. Sigourney immediately rejected this view. She saw Shylock as an unorthodox businessman and nothing more. As for the racial problems, these were merely part of the story, and a historically accurate representation of the times. Regardless of this opinion, the new production was almost certain to court controversy. For Sigourney the risk of outbursts would only be a trifling inconvenience in the face of her main objective: to prove to herself that she could succeed in a classical role after the embarrassing *Macbeth* escapade. This time around Sigourney was tackling another difficult Shakespearean woman: Portia.

Show business couples working together can often spell disaster. Sometimes marital and personal problems can creep into the rehearsal room, causing friction and a poor working atmosphere. The pressures inherent in putting on a show can add to the strain of married life, especially when both the husband and wife are working and living together twenty-four hours a day. There is no neutral party to go home to and discuss the joys or heartaches of the day. Luckily working on *The Merchant of Venice* wasn't that much of a burden on the Simpsons' fledgling marriage. But there were problems, namely that Sigourney felt her husband was far tougher on her during rehearsals than any other cast member. But the experience was an enjoyable one. 'I think he is a wonderful director,' she told *Cable Guide* magazine in July 1987. 'So I married well.' Thoughts of a re-match, however, were greeted less enthusiastically by Sigourney. 'I'm not sure he wants to work with me again. I think he found me difficult.' In common with most of her theatrical work, *The Merchant of Venice* was presented off-Broadway, this time at the CSC Repertory on Manhattan's Lower East Side. Sadly the play was heavily panned. 'We got killed,' Sigourney confessed to *Première* magazine in October 1988. 'I didn't even read the reviews, but I know we got killed.' Some of the notices were unjustifiably harsh, others were downright rude. The *New York Post* wrote: 'Let not the Bard's quality be strained, but lo it has!' However, the play continued a fairly profitable run until mid-January 1987.

Even the disastrous reception for *The Merchant of Venice* did little to harm Sigourney's renewed prominence in the movie world. After two disappointing films, *Aliens* had catapulted her back into the running for top female box-office draw. But yet again she had little time for the superficial trappings of fame. She still made a point of staying away from Hollywood as much as she could. She did not want to be treated like a cosseted starlet, chauffeur-driven to lunch and the hairdresser's in a limousine the length of a block, constantly surrounded by a staff of helpers blindly obeying her every command. 'That is the sure road to neurosis, and one I fight to stay clear of.'

11 *Gorilla Tactics*

Sigourney Weaver stood perfectly still. She knew that any movement on her part could mean certain death. Out of the bush, with a hoot and a beating of its chest, had emerged a huge silverback gorilla, the dominant male of the ape family that Sigourney had just disturbed. In the mind of the animal this woman was a threatening force and had to be dealt with. Her blood turned cold as the majestic creature moved ominously closer, fur bristling, back arched, and fierceness etched on its face. Sigourney was fully aware of the gorilla's power. If it so desired this male could trample her underfoot with ease, or club her to death with those giant hands in seconds. She sensed a rush of panic invade her body. 'When you have four hundred pounds of pissed off gorilla inching up on you, you start seeing your life flash by.' But the actress kept her poise, stood her ground and assumed the submissive position that her African tracker had taught her. She was told that as soon as she stopped looking threatening the ape would back off. Sure enough, the animal quickly lost interest in Sigourney and nonchalantly stalked past her and disappeared back into the bush. The long chain of events leading up to her predicament must have flooded to Sigourney's mind at that perilous moment. Sigourney found herself asking why she was crouching on top of a 12-thousand-feet mountain in Central Africa risking life and limb amongst a group of wild gorillas – apart from having the time of her life. The answer lies in the life of an extraordinary woman, Dian Fossey.

The achievements of this established maverick are well documented, as are the circumstances which led to her untimely and tragic end. In 1967 Dian Fossey travelled to the African province of Rwanda where she studied the dwindling population of the mountain gorilla. For eighteen years she lived amongst these graceful animals and due to the coverage her research received in the *National Geographic*, she became one of the most cherished and controversial animal conservationists in modern times, radically altering the world's perception of the gorilla. (Previously the world had categorized these animals as ferocious and savage. She saw that they were friendly, noble creatures, only violent when threatened.) She helped to save the species from extinction. Her accomplishments are all the more remarkable when one considers that she never received any formal scientific training and was unqualified as a zoologist. But the Fossey story has a dark side. She lived in appallingly primitive conditions, in near-solitude and was immersed in her work to the point of obsession. She also made many enemies and incurred the wrath of the local Bahutu tribe and numerous government officials because of her one-woman crusade against the poachers who slaughtered the gorillas for profit, turning their hands into chic ashtrays, their heads into trophies, and selling their young to zoos. In this vicious personal war Fossey unleashed her own reign of terror, sometimes using ruthless methods. She wasn't above staging mock executions; playing on tribal superstition by posing as a witch; burning down native huts; and shooting stray cattle that wandered into *her* domain. She was completely and utterly pro-animal. Anyone who came near her gorillas was seen as a threat. Not surprisingly, the general consensus was that she had gone completely insane. One evening just after Christmas in 1985, an unknown assailant crept into Fossey's home and hacked her to death as she lay on her bed resting. Although the murder remains a mystery, suspicions point to vengeful poachers as the culprits, or a conspiracy formulated by the upper echelons of government. Whatever, she rests in peace now, buried on her animal reserve next to the graves of her beloved gorillas.

At the time of Fossey's death, plans were already under way to make a film about her life, based on her own book. (Dian once told friends that she wanted Brooke Shields and Elizabeth Taylor to portray her at different ages.) On Boxing Day 1985 producer Arnold Glimcher arrived in Rwanda to visit Fossey, who had agreed to be a consultant on the movie.

But Fossey was butchered, as Glimcher slept off the effects of his long plane journey at a hotel in Kigali, Rwanda's capital. The following morning the mountain where Fossey's research centre was located was sealed off as an investigation into the brutal killing began. Glimcher was reluctantly forced to admit defeat. After the sudden death of Fossey there seemed no future for his project. But the producer remained in Rwanda for a week, interviewing Fossey's friends and co-workers. He believed he had uncovered a multi-layered complexity to the woman's life that had scarcely been touched upon in her autobiography. The potential existed for a picture that not only told the story of Fossey's work but delved deep into the psyche of a woman prepared to forsake her country, a fiancé, and a conventional family life, for the wild, untamed jungles of Africa. Meanwhile, back in Los Angeles, Warner Bros. were already planning to make their own version of the Fossey story and had hired Bob Rafelson to direct *Heaven and Earth: The Tragic Life and Death of Dian Fossey*, with Ann-Margaret in the lead. Blissfully unaware of the mounting competition, Glimcher had won the backing of Universal and the search for a suitable director for his project began in earnest. The two opposing studios first learnt of one another's intentions when their representatives met quite by chance in a hotel lobby in Kigali. Both studios eventually agreed to share the costs and jointly produce Glimcher's *Gorillas in the Mist*. Bob Rafelson was dropped because he wanted to portray Fossey as a raving lunatic. Another director was urgently required; shooting had to begin early in July before the torrential rains started in September. Under consideration were James Cameron, Richard Donner, and Oliver Stone (who was keen on the idea but was already committed to making *Wall Street*). Finally, British director Michael Apted was selected. Like Glimcher, Apted was interested in making an uplifting picture, 'not a film about a crank'. Apted's familiarity with the documentary genre (Granada Television's *28 Up* and Sting's *Bring on the Night*), and his feature work (*Stardust, The Coalminer's Daughter, Gorky Park*), held him in good stead for a movie that merged fact and fiction in a quasi-documentary form.

The most troublesome pre-production chore was finding an appropriate actress to play Fossey. Practically every major female star in Hollywood wanted the role. Sigourney Weaver quickly established herself as the leading contender after Jessica Lange, the producer's first choice, became pregnant. Both studios agreed that Sigourney was perfect. In Apted's estimation Sigourney was one of only six or seven actresses in the world who could have got a company to finance such an uncommercial property and had the strength and presence to succeed. Sigourney's name had held a certain cachet in the decade since *Alien*, but that special role to launch her into the realms of real stardom had remained frustratingly elusive. *Gorillas in the Mist* was a belated godsend in that respect. Sigourney sensed that Dian Fossey could be her 'great' role, her *Hamlet*. In the words of Apted, 'She was born to play this part. She fell into it so naturally.' But at first Weaver was hesitant about how the film-makers were going to treat Fossey's life. Sigourney had read her book some years before and felt then that the story didn't constitute good cinematic material. The last thing the actress wanted to do was get involved in some glossy Hollywood fairy tale. Early talk about concentrating the film on Fossey's sad and lonely descent into madness also caused Sigourney distress. She didn't see Dian's single-mindedness about her 'cause' as a sign of insanity. She and Apted were more interested in showing on screen a woman of courage and staggering achievements, to make her philosophy and passion available to a wider audience. They do not totally ignore the murky aspect of her life. Although the film is deeply prejudiced in Fossey's favour, Apted often shows her in an unflattering light. The final dark scenes are among the film's finest as we see her fall into an abyss of despair of her own making and wonder if the bruised, fanatical woman, reprimanding politicians and wealthy poachers, and torturing her enemies, is not 'going ape' herself. It is a tribute to Sigourney's performance and Apted's careful direction that they have the courage to de-glamorize their subject.

As Weaver, Apted, Glimcher, and writer Anna Hamilton Phelan were in London putting the finishing touches to the script, the big studios in Los Angeles were getting cold feet. And who could blame them? They were about to spend $27 million to send a film crew to six extinct volcanoes on the Virunga mountain range in an African country where no motion picture had ever been made. Memories of the *Lone Star* fiasco must have flooded back when Sigourney heard the news. Here was another film she truly believed in that was on the verge of being scrapped. Whilst in London, Glimcher was told that Warner and Universal had decided not to go ahead with the movie because the whole enterprise was just too expensive a risk. But all was not lost. Glimcher organized a frantic meeting and a phone campaign, by the end of which a vast proportion of the crew had consented to work for lower salaries. He telephoned Sigourney, who immediately agreed to defer one third of her fee. Nearly $3 million was trimmed from the budget. The movie was back on.

Sigourney took great pleasure in filling the part of Fossey out with as much detail as she could. The actress studied hours of film footage of the woman, analysing her body movements and gestures in much the same way as Fossey herself had learned how to mimic her beloved gorillas. She read every news clipping and book she could lay her hands on in an effort to foster an understanding of Dian's character and motivation. As the research continued apace Sigourney found herself completely entranced by Fossey and shocked by the harsh contrasts that existed in her life. She was a creature of opposites, seen by many as a great scientist and by others as a charlatan. Fossey was capable of caring and tender moments; while at other times, particularly towards the end of her life, she was a foul-mouthed, hard-drinking, chain-smoking bitch. The complexity of the woman was fascinating. During filming, Dian Fossey became part of Sigourney's life. She is prone to become obsessive about the characters she plays and once they are gone she can miss their company for months. The ghost of Dian Fossey took a lot longer to exorcize mainly because of her death and the cause for which she fought. Not only was Fossey the most demanding role of Sigourney's career to date but she was also quite unique: this woman had actually once lived, she was no fanciful creation conceived by some writer's despot imagination. 'She was a complex subject and I really wanted to play a real woman, something incredible to act.' For some years now, Sigourney had expressed a desire to play a real-life character, a historical figure, someone like Georgia O'Keefe or Amelia Earhart. Sigourney had been impressed by Meryl

Streep's interpretation of Isak Dinesen in *Out of Africa*, which she classed as one of her finest performances. But she didn't want such a film to turn into a star vehicle; she hated the idea of appearing in a movie where the whole purpose of the project was to give the actress a big part. She would always prefer to play a small part within a company of capable actors than the leading role in a turkey. But, as with *Aliens*, Sigourney was once again burdened with the awesome responsibility of carrying a major movie single-handed. Although consistently upstaged by her primate co-stars, if Sigourney were to give a bad performance, irrespective of the film's other sparkling merits, *Gorillas in the Mist* would have fallen flat on its face.

There was a spark of adventure in the heart of Sigourney Weaver as she reclined in her comfortable airline seat, full of excitement and expectancy about her trip to Africa and what would be the most incredible three months of her life. She felt relatively pleased with all the preparatory work she had been able to do on Fossey and the two weeks of mountain training she had endured in Hawaii to strengthen her for the rigours of location filming in Rwanda. Just prior to leaving America Sigourney was asked by *Life* magazine if she would record her thoughts and experiences in the form of a daily diary which the periodical would then publish. Normally publicity-shy, she agreed to the request and her article became an invaluable account of the filming of *Gorillas in the Mist* and a fitting tribute to the memory and work of Dian Fossey. Mixed in with all the excitement was a certain amount of trepidation. 'I worry to death about each new thing. When I had to go off to Africa I acted like I was going off to join the Foreign Legion for twenty years,' Sigourney told *You* magazine in November 1989. The actress was still unsure how the gorillas were going to react to her. The entire production rested on the interplay between the star and the animals. If there was no magical spark between them there would be no movie.

Principal photography on *Gorillas in the Mist* began on 2 July 1987, close to Fossey's Karisoke Research Centre and her sad, lonely grave. Sigourney found working so close to where Fossey had actually lived an inspiration. On one occasion she thought it would be an interesting and beneficial exercise to visit Fossey's small and unpretentious home. This was a serious mistake. The experience deeply upset the actress and left her devastated for days afterwards. Once inside, Sigourney had walked into the very room where Dian had met her death. All her personal belongings were still there and the mattress on which she was murdered still bore her bloodstains. 'I'm not a great believer in psychic phenomena, but I felt something evil had happened there.'

Working with wild animals is highly dangerous and unpredictable, not least when one is dealing with so rare a creature as the mountain gorilla. Sigourney was naturally apprehensive about meeting the apes for the first time. Her fears were manifold: would the gorillas accept her, would she know what to do and, most worrying of all, would she panic? But the thrill of following in the footsteps of Dian Fossey bolstered her spirit. On that magical first trip to see the gorillas she was accompanied by David Watts, who currently ran the research centre. Trudging through vast vegetation they located a gorilla family close to Dian's grave. Their presence was detected by Watts when he heard 'pok, pok, pok, pok, pok', the distinctive sound of the male beating his chest; and the tell-tale noise of the apes chewing on foliage. Suddenly, there in front of Sigourney was a mammoth silverback, staring down at her like a king before a humble subject. 'I don't think I ever looked back after that,' she told *Interview* magazine in July 1988. 'It was like walking into a forest and seeing a unicorn.' Sigourney steadied herself and crouched down among the undergrowth. Suddenly a young female, Jozi, waddled up towards the actress and sat beside her. Sigourney's heart began to beat hysterically as she battled to contain her excitement. Never before had she been so close to a wild animal. In that single moment all of Sigourney's fears and anxieties melted away. The tiny gorilla next to her seemed so friendly and innocently curious as it reached over to study her camera. Jozi then leaned up against Sigourney and began to quiz her strange white face. Weaver had been taught basic gorilla etiquette by an African tracker and knew the importance of not looking directly into the eyes of an ape. But emotions were running high and the temptation was too great to resist meeting Jozi's inquisitive gaze. Among those gorillas, many of which Fossey herself had studied, Sigourney felt at peace, almost at home. 'There was nowhere in the world I wanted to be more than right there.' Sigourney was fully aware of how fortunate she was to be in such close proximity to these precious and free animals and never took the intimacy she developed with some of the gorillas for granted; every meeting carried with it a subtle air of apprehension. After her first encounter with the apes Weaver knew that she had come on a 'very long journey and the result was a feeling of pure unalloyed joy, of a kind which I haven't felt before or since'. Oneness with the gorillas was the key to Dian Fossey's character's caged soul.

Less of a pleasure were the near-primitive conditions cast and crew were forced to endure. There was no telephone, no television, no mail service, in fact hardly any modern facilities at all. The production relied heavily on several hundred Rwandans who acted as a kind of human lifeline to the outside world, bringing in food, supplies and information. Accommodation was also rather crude; no four-star hotels here. Instead, everyone slept in tents on rickety cots whose four legs stood in bowls of water to prevent ants from crawling up and joining them in bed. But for the most part Sigourney held Rwanda in reverence. It was a hauntingly beautiful country despite sinister parallels to the Philippines, where she had made *The Year of Living Dangerously* five years before. Rwanda was a rough place. The soldiers all carried guns and usually resorted to cracking people over the head with their rifle butts if anyone got in the way. The army were so paranoid that they thought the film crew were mercenaries.

Apted's base camp was situated at the foot of Fossey's mountain and each day Sigourney and the crew had to climb up the steep slopes in search of the gorillas living at extremely high altitudes at least two or three hours away. Once the team had to walk eight hours before finding them. Conditions were horrendous: the temperature was constantly shifting from hot to cold, and it invariably rained. Because of the strict rules imposed on the production by the local authorities only a maximum of six people were allowed near the gorillas at any one time. Such restrictions created formidable problems. The film unit had to be stripped to a bare minimum (even Apted had to occasionally double as assistant cameraman), and everyone had to carry their own equipment up the mountain. There were no roads and helicopter lifts were banned.

During the course of filming the astonishing rapport between Sigourney and the gorillas prospered. She grew more confident in their presence and would spend hours at a time crouching in the long grass with the apes, adopting their gestures, munching on some shrubs with them, as Dian had done, and even learning their special talk, a combination of body language and belching. She was taught to be in a submissive posture when she was with the apes, especially when the dominant male was around, and never to run if one of them charged: she was to stand her ground. Sigourney was also advised to keep her hands clasped over her neck. This was to prevent a bite through the jugular vein. (One cameraman was severely bitten while attempting to take a close-up.) Luckily, Sigourney was able to keep out of trouble, although she was once slapped hard across the shoulder by one of the gorillas. This was not done in any malicious way; it was really a form of communication. If the animal had really wanted to harm Sigourney she wouldn't have been able to stand. Sometimes she was worried that she might do something inadvertently to scare the apes, but David Watts was always on hand to guide the actress from the gorillas who might have been dangerous, to those who revelled in the company of people. To achieve some of the more intimate shots of Sigourney and the gorillas, a small transmitter was placed in her ear through which she was coached in a series of hair-raising situations. In this way some truly amazing scenes were achieved without putting the actress in any unnecessary danger. About midway through the filming, Sigourney became adept at recognizing all the gorillas and identifying their individual personalities. She had her favourites, of course, like Maggie, a quaint female who was very friendly. Others were less hospitable. One huge gorilla called Pablo was known to have dragged women down the mountain. But Sigourney quickly learnt that if she sat next to Ziz, the huge silverback that the actress described as 'a 450-pound version of Rodin's "The Thinker" with a head the size of a boulder', then Pablo never bothered her. And there was Shinda, perhaps the most boisterous of the group, who seemed to flirt openly with Sigourney.

During those three months of location filming in Africa, Apted and his crew managed to capture on camera some truly unique shots of the gorillas interacting with Sigourney Weaver. These he would later call 'the heartbeat of the movie'. A great deal of patience was required in order to achieve these results. Often the crew had to wait for hours to see what the apes were going to do. These were not performing animals who acted the natural history specimen on cue. Scenes were often dictated by the behaviour of the gorillas on a certain day of filming. Sigourney found such unpredictability stimulating, and her working relationship with the apes was almost on a level with improvisation. Occasionally the hours of waiting did try her slender patience, but those wonderful shared moments with Maggie, Ziz, and the others made the whole venture more than worthwhile. The gorillas had a profound effect on everyone who worked on the film; no one left untouched by the experience. Watching the wild mountain gorillas living in their natural habitat, eating, playing with their young, and generally enjoying life, is something Sigourney will never forget. She especially loved playing with the young gorillas. They were sometimes so enthusiastic that they crawled all over her. One of the mothers would always be on hand just to make sure no harm came to them, although it was usually the other way round. The gorilla young had a nasty habit of swinging on Sigourney's pigtails causing her excruciating pain. But these were joyous and cherished moments. 'Roaming around with their babies all day made me realize how much I wanted a child of my own.'

Before her marriage reliance on men had never been one of Sigourney's weaknesses. She and Jim Simpson are regularly parted because of work commitments. 'We don't like being away from each other, it seems to defeat the whole purpose of living.' Sigourney's participation in *Gorillas in the Mist* meant nearly four months apart. Under normal circumstances she would never have tolerated such a separation, but the Fossey film was different. For that summer the couple were just going to have to grin and bear it. In any case Jim had a great deal of theatrical work back home in America to keep him occupied, which helped ease Sigourney's guilty conscience. He also managed to visit his wife three times in Africa. For Sigourney these were welcome breaks away from the basic living conditions and near-isolation that were beginning to take their toll. The couple try hard to balance their professional and private lives and manage to see a surprising amount of each other. 'We have long periods of time together when we leave the city and go away just to be with each other,' Sigourney told *Woman's Journal* in December 1988. 'We do have separations, but I'm sure I see more of him than some wives do who work nine to five at an office job.'

When the time came to leave the jungle and the gorillas and fly to London and Shepperton Studios for interior work, Sigourney's heart was in danger of breaking. She felt like she was leaving behind old friends. Her extraordinary rapport with the gorillas won her the admiration of everyone concerned with the picture. Glimcher thought Sigourney was the bravest actress he had ever known, and couldn't think of anyone else who could have played the part so well. 'She's not a primadonna,' Glimcher told *Films and Filming* in March 1989. 'She's very relaxed and creative around a crew. She never complains and is absolutely indefatigable.' Apted greatly admired the courage Sigourney showed every time she came into contact with the gorillas. In the middle of possible danger she was as steady as a rock, whatever her inner fears might have been. 'She had an uncanny feel for the animals,' Apted recalled. Unquestionably, the highest compliment came from Roz Carr, who was one of Fossey's closest friends in Rwanda. After viewing the film she was in awe of Weaver's performance. 'Sigourney is perfect as Dian, and I'm so grateful for that. She's really made herself into a second Dian. It's quite remarkable.' Others who were close to Fossey all agreed that Sigourney had captured the woman's essence memorably.

That October Sigourney returned to Rwanda to visit the gorilla group, eager to find out whether or not they still remembered her. Along with a group of guides and a trusty film crew Sigourney walked up the familiar path of Fossey's mountain gallantly trying to keep a tight rein on her emotions. In a clearing they came across the gorillas who casually strolled past her without the merest hint of recognition. Perhaps it was wrong of Sigourney to have expected some kind of human response from the gorillas. They are very independent creatures, they care for little else but their own group. Still, she couldn't help but feel bitterly disappointed and hurt. Then Maggie came over and laid her warm hand on Sigourney's shoulder and squeezed it gently. Sigourney burst into tears, they rolled down her cheeks, and she had to turn her face away from the camera in embarrassment. It was clear that Maggie, in her own way, had just said, 'Hi.' 'That's why I don't want to let too much time go by before I go back. I always want to go back.'

Filming *Gorillas in the Mist* and working so closely with the apes and animal conservationists changed Sigourney's outlook on life dramatically. The actress became a champion for animal rights and began to call for the preservation of all endangered species. She also developed a heightened awareness of ecological issues in general. For example, she no longer expressed a desire to visit zoos: they were places she now called prisons. 'I think I now see gorillas as our fellow creatures in the way Dian did,' Sigourney told *Films and Filming* in March 1989. 'One of our great mistakes is that humans think of the world as their planet and take animals for granted.' Although Sigourney became actively involved in the Fossey preservation cause, director Michael Apted remained virtually unaffected by his African ordeal, and totally indifferent to the mountain gorilla who, in his considered opinion only seemed to 'fart, fuck and eat'. To him the film had wider implications. It was less about the fate of one endangered species, and more about how humankind treats all wildlife, how we are slowly destroying the earth, and what we are handing on to future generations. (*Gorillas in the Mist* emerged at a time of increased awareness about the environment and green issues.) Sigourney has now adopted Maggie and sends regular donations to the Karisoke Centre, continuing in her own way the invaluable work started by Dian Fossey. 'I know there are many priorities in the world but I believe trying to save a species may help us to understand and save ourselves,' Sigourney said to *You* magazine in January 1989. The Digit Fund, named after the huge silverback gorilla that befriended Fossey and who was brutally slain by poachers, was set up to aid the mountain gorillas of Rwanda. The fund runs a scheme where people can adopt gorillas and Sigourney is heavily involved, as making television appeals on behalf of the project.

Over the last few years Sigourney has been working with other charities. One of the few saving graces of her celebrity status is that she can call attention to certain political issues. In the latter half of 1986 she spoke at the Lawyers Committee for Human Rights benefit honouring Mrs Aquino. Sigourney was proud to be involved with the group which, like Amnesty International, was a non-partisan organization that investigated human rights violations by governments of all political persuasions. Perhaps due to the very nature of their work actors tend to be very sensitive about humanitarian issues. 'We look into individual souls. We care about human beings.' Sigourney disclosed to *Film Comment* in December 1986. 'If you don't, you don't become an actor.' Making science fiction films has also taught her that the human race are a species, not a collection of ethnic groups and nationalities. If the actress could take world citizenship tomorrow she would. 'Though I'm very glad to be American.'

In mid-1988 Sigourney attended a huge AIDS benefit with Christopher Durang. This is another cause that the actress feels very strongly about. AIDS had a devastating effect on the entertainment industry and she is only too painfully aware of the cruel realities of the disease, having known colleagues struck down by it. At the beginning of the AIDS epidemic Sigourney was bitter about all the fallacies that built up about it being purely a gay plague and all the paranoia that swelled up as a consequence. 'It really makes me angry that people are so afraid, but many people just don't know anyone with AIDS,' Sigourney told *Interview* magazine in July 1988. 'When you actually see someone with AIDS you feel you want to reach out to them – They're ill. Thank goodness I'm not afraid anymore, but it's still so sad.'

Gorillas in the Mist opened in America in September 1988. Sigourney's performance was unanimously acclaimed wherever the film played and she justly deserved her second Oscar nomination. Coincidentally she was also nominated the same year for her supporting role in *Working Girl*.

Sigourney was widely tipped to snatch the top award, but ended up losing both. She was naturally flattered that her work had been acknowledged by the academy, but was disappointed to lose out twice in the same evening. But a Golden Globe award for Best Actress proved ample compensation. Sigourney attended the ceremony in a seductive red dress and posed for photographers with the male winner, Dustin Hoffman. In London, *Gorillas in the Mist* opened in late January 1989 at a royal charity première. Sigourney flew into the capital with her husband to attend the glitzy affair and was greatly pleased by the British critics' favourable reaction to the film. Many applauded her portrayal. 'Remarkable true story, strengthened by Sigourney Weaver's playing, a low-key but towering performance,' said the *Daily Mail*. 'Handsome, absorbing and honourable, Weaver is superb,' spoke the *Sunday Telegraph*.

Gorillas in the Mist is Sigourney's favourite film. Along with *The Year of Living Dangerously*, she feels the picture has something important and valid to express. For her personally, it was an incredible working experience. Certainly the role of Dian Fossey is Sigourney's most rewarding to date. The film even managed to do some global good – educating people about the gorillas. It also raised the rate of tourism to Rwanda. Provided this is carefully regulated, all that western money pouring in will help build a future for the mountain gorillas. Sigourney was also invited to the United Nations to accept a posthumous medal on behalf of Dian Fossey from the president of Rwanda. Even today she feels honoured and privileged to have been entrusted with the awesome obligation of playing Fossey on screen. 'I feel like I've finally gone legit.' Weaver could now build on this and use the worldwide popularity of the movie and the personal acclaim she received as a bargaining chip in her desire to work with more challenging material.

12 *Working Girl*

Ten full years had elapsed since Sigourney Weaver's dramatic breakthrough in *Alien*. In the interim she had worked with some of the best actors and directors in the business and was now a universally respected actress, a star worthy of an Oscar nomination, and a sex symbol. 1989 brought with it a kind of contentment that Sigourney had never known before. Her personal and professional lives seemed at last in true harmony. Her marriage to Jim Simpson was still as fresh and loving as ever. And the potent combination of critical acclaim for and box-office success of her last two pictures had finally exalted her to a level shared by Meryl Streep. For Sigourney's legion of devoted admirers, her elevation to superstar status had been long overdue. Once again she was hot property. Sigourney has acquired what so few women are able to in the film business: power. While all her movies may not be blockbusters, she is highly regarded and popular throughout the world, primarily because of the astonishing recognition she has achieved via *Ghostbusters* and the *Alien* series. Sigourney is the guarantee which enables producers to obtain the necessary financial backing for their film projects. Few female stars have such pull in Hollywood. But perhaps the time had come for her to relax and abandon ambition, temporarily, channelling her immense energy into family life instead.

An offer in the early months of 1988 to play a small role in *Working Girl* (a pleasantly enjoyable romantic comedy with a sound old-fashioned base), arrived at exactly the right time for Sigourney. Her previous two films had been real epics and her roles in them were monumentally tough and demanding. The idea of playing a supporting role for once and letting another actress take on the responsibility of carrying the movie was certainly appealing. The film's New York location was a further enticement. After her strenuous exertions in the mountains of central Africa it would be a welcome change to make a film practically on her own doorstep. She wouldn't have far to travel to get to the various location sites and, at the end of a day's filming, unlike her fellow actors and crew members who were put up in hotels away from their loved ones, Sigourney was never far away from home and Jim Simpson. 'I accepted because I got to wear pretty clothes and sleep in my own bed at night.' The only drawback was her own reservation about playing film comedy again, especially after her horrendous experiences on *Deal of the Century* and *A Woman or Two*. Sigourney wanted to wait for the right part, and the right director: Mike Nichols, for example. Ever since their fruitful Broadway collaboration on *Hurlyburly* Sigourney had been anxious to work with him again. The part Nichols was offering her in *Working Girl* was a pure gem, a character quite unlike any she had yet personified on screen. Admittedly Katharine Parker was another beautiful and ultra-intelligent eighties woman, but she was also utterly ruthless and ice-cold. Katharine is the ultimate super-bitch executive. A male nightmare, she exudes sophistication and class, dressing with powerful purposefulness, and is not averse to wiping out anyone who threatens her exulted, yet tenuous, position with callous efficiency. The story concerns Tess (Melanie Griffith), an innocent, but capable, Girl-Friday secretary who is determined to pull herself out of the typing pool and become an executive. Unfortunately, she lacks Ivy League credentials and social gloss. In *Working Girl* Nichols dismantles the myth that America is a classless society. Both Tess and Katharine are exact contemporaries; the only difference between them is privilege. Tess is appalled to discover that Katharine has purloined one of her business ideas, passing it off as her own. When Katharine is incapacitated by a skiing accident Tess fills her executive chair and begins an earnest assault on the corporate ladder, stealing Katharine's boyfriend, played by Harrison Ford, into the bargain.

Katharine Parker was hardly a crowd-pleasing role. Audiences in America were not above booing the heartless character. When Sigourney was told about the effect her portrayal was having on audiences she found it all quite amusing. 'I think just about everybody in America now hates me,' she joked. (As a result of her deliciously sinister performance as the bitchy Katharine Parker, she was offered a couple of really nasty, villainous roles, which she seriously considered playing. 'I kinda like being a baddie,' she confessed.) Sigourney was delighted that her performance had provoked such a huge response from the American public and even admitted to having a soft spot for Katharine. Sigourney's preparatory work prior to playing the character, as usual, was an extensive process. Sigourney's research took her deep into the financial nerve-centre of New York where she visited some of the city's major brokerage houses and met with some of Wall Street's top female executives. Thanks to the cooperation of the city fathers Nichols and his crew were allowed to film within the normally secretive world of big business, and completely on location (no studio sets were utilized). Filming began in mid-February 1988, with New York in the freezing grip of another harsh winter. For the workplace no fewer than four contrasting buildings were used. The vast secretarial pool was a single set constructed over three weeks from scratch on the twenty-first floor of a mammoth skyscraper on the tip of lower Manhattan.

Visiting Wall Street and becoming acquainted with this whole new world was a fascinating insight into what goes on behind the closed doors of corporate America. This was a part of New York Sigourney had never bothered to investigate before. She found the pace and pressures of high finance intoxicating, to say the least. 'It is so much more competitive than say show-business.' Often Sigourney would be allowed to sit in on board meetings, watching and listening attentively. She would also follow chosen female executives around on their daily schedules, familiarizing herself with how they conducted themselves and coped with stressful situations. She also met for lunch, and had drinks with, key people in business to glean as much information as she could about their life style and personalities. A lot of the women Sigourney encountered, who had attained a high corporate position, tended to keep quiet about their own particular achievements, perhaps because they were still self-conscious about how they were being perceived in the firm by their fellow workers, both male and female. Sigourney also discovered that people like Katharine Parker really did exist. All the female executives that she interviewed told stories on each other. 'I think there was a little bit of Katharine in all of them.'

In some respects the character of Katharine Parker was the mirror-image of Sigourney. Maybe this was why she liked and quietly admired her so much. Both had gone to the right schools and were from rich, society backgrounds. Their personalities reeked of the Ivy League. Just like Katharine, Sigourney was brought up 'to feel that whenever I spoke I was worth listening to'. Katharine feels entitled to stamp over everyone; she's certain that the power is better off in the hands of people such as herself. As a child, Sigourney herself was continually being told that she was special, and in the top two per cent of the social strata. 'I didn't feel guilty about it,' Sigourney told *Today* newspaper in January 1989. 'And neither does Katharine Parker.' Although parallels do exist between the two women in terms of background and upbringing, they share few adult attributes, apart from an ambitious drive. Her upper class breeding often works against Sigourney career-wise. But in the case of *Working Girl* this was exactly what Nichols wanted and the director actively encouraged her to take on the part.

Sigourney plays Parker with winning comic style. Her portrayal is a joy to watch, especially the scenes where she lies in a hospital bed with her leg in plaster after the accident, eternally on the phone and ordering the hospital staff around like slaves; or her delicious feigning of intimacy and office sisterhood with Tess. There's also a lovely in-joke when Katharine returns in crutches from her ski 'break' holding a large cuddly toy gorilla: a comic reminder of Sigourney's previous cinematic role. Unfortunately, in the latter stages of the movie Nichols turns Katharine into a figure of fun, a caricature. One's sympathies tend to float towards her at the end when her ruse is uncovered and she is ridiculed by all and sundry and fired on the spot. Nichols blatantly set her up as a ball-breaking career bitch. Ultimately, Katharine is punished just for behaving too much like a man. *Working Girl* opened in America on 21 December 1988 and proved enormously popular with the public, amassing $60 million at the box-office. In England, Sigourney received critical acclaim for her role as the viperish Katharine. 'A tough-fibred, scene stealing performance. It's a water-tight role and she coasts to glory on it,' said the *Daily Express*; while the *Daily Telegraph* called the characterization 'a bold and brilliant parody'. Her performance won the Best Supporting Actress award at the Golden Globes in January 1989, a ceremony Sigourney seems always to do well at. She also received an Oscar nomination in the same category. The film itself fared surprisingly well with a bag of six nominations, including Best Film.

But the film was not well received everywhere. Alarm-bells sounded in feminist quarters. They objected strongly to many of Nichols' views. 'If feminists are going to object to me playing a ruthless woman sympathetically all I can say is I don't care,' Weaver told *Today* newspaper. 'There are a lot of people like Katharine out there and it's not my responsibility if others don't like that.' The film had unintentionally touched a raw nerve in US society, and struck a chord in the corridors of corporate America because the message it preached was true. Many people saw Nichols' work as a warning about how women are being turned into power-broking monsters. Women's liberation has allowed Hollywood to put on the screen a female fiend as evil and tyrannical as any fictional *femme fatale* or Jezebel. At last, female high-flyers are winning the top jobs they have long deserved, but such emancipation has resulted in even the most intelligent women taking on the aggressively scheming characteristics of the worst male company shark. In the eyes of Hollywood, these new career women are the more deadly of the species: their cold ruthlessness is well hidden beneath expensive fashion-wear, the smell of their venom is sweetened by the scent of Chanel No. 5. Such a reputation is perhaps unfair, but even in the caring nineties many successful women continue to be branded as more tough, ambitious, and conniving than their male counterparts. Women still feel compelled to fight among themselves for the token top job and the other assorted scraps that are all too infrequently thrown to them. And once they have achieved some professional status they often have to work twice as hard as the man both to gain and maintain their position. 'I still hope that women can be better than men,' Sigourney believes. 'As naïve as that may sound.'

Sigourney Weaver's battleground is Hollywood. During the release of *Working Girl* she unwittingly stirred up a hornet's nest when she publicly demanded equal pay with male stars. She used her prominence as one of America's leading female celebrities to lend weight to the argument that male actors are paid proportionally too much for their services. (A state of affairs mirrored in other lines of work). Sigourney cited *Working Girl* as a prime example. Both she and Melanie Griffith were paid about half Harrison Ford's fee. She wanted it to be known that this kind of discrimination happened on every film and to every leading actress, going right back to the old studio system when every female star suffered enormous inequality. Not much had altered in Hollywood in the intervening years. Women were still at the bottom of the barrel in terms of financial reward. Sigourney eventually decided that, to guarantee her income, she would have to work for herself. Today, like Barbra Streisand, she owns her own production company, christened Goat Cay and based in New York, a potent indication of her increasing significance in American cinema. The actress hopes in the near future to begin nurturing and developing her own film projects. One of her early plans was to adapt a Yukio Mishima play for screen and theatre under the direction of her husband. 'I'm having a wonderful time producing,' Sigourney disclosed to a journalist in 1990. 'There are good producers and bad producers. I've learned the hard way what not to do. The ultimate aim is to produce things I'm not actually in. I'm not looking for vehicles for myself. It's not a vanity company.'

Going back to Hollywood pay-scaling, one can argue that the reason that stars like Harrison Ford and some of the other major male actors receive larger salaries than Hollywood's female actors is because of their greater box-office appeal. They are far more popular with mass audiences, on the whole, than their female counterparts. It is argued that, because they are largely responsible for attracting the public into movie theatres, they surely deserve the better fees. That might be true, but in the last decade men's wages have gone into orbit. People like Schwarzenegger and Tom Cruise pocket astronomical amounts of money, particularly for sequel work. When Sigourney agreed to return as Ripley in *Aliens* she was paid just $1 million. Yet if Paul Newman, the producer's first choice in *Alien* (or any other big male star) had played the original role and was then enticed back, they would have demanded and received five times that sum. One of Sigourney's ambitions is to organize twenty of the biggest female 'names', people like Meryl Streep, Glenn Close, and Michelle Pfeiffer, into some kind of protest movement that would force a change in the rules. 'Wouldn't it be fun? The twenty of us bucking the system.'

When the sequel to the hugely successful *Ghostbusters* opened in America in the summer of 1989 no one was really surprised: such an eventuality was as inevitable as Christmas. Cinemagoers were far more curious about just why the follow-up had taken five years to reach the screen. The late eighties was the age of the sequel, and each summer a profusion of them would be released to fight it out for box-office glory. When *Ghostbusters 2* opened in June the main competition was from other follow-ups like *Indiana Jones and the Last Crusade*, *Star Trek V*, *Lethal Weapon 2* and the sixteenth James Bond movie.

There were two factors that contributed to the unusually long delay in getting *Ghostbusters 2* rolling, namely Bill Murray and David Puttnam. In the summer of 1986 Puttnam became the head of Columbia Pictures. His troubled time in the hot seat has been well documented, but perhaps less well known is the independent British producer's stubborn unwillingness to even entertain thoughts of making a *Ghostbusters* sequel. At Columbia, Puttnam's dream was to concentrate on producing relatively low and medium cost pictures of quality. A sequel to *Ghostbusters* would be neither cheap nor of a particularly high quality. The original film had been the biggest hit in Columbia's history, however, and many people felt dismay over Puttnam's blank refusal to allow the sequel to go ahead. He further angered them by suggesting that the film be made with an all-new and lower-salaried cast. There was also a much publicized rift between Puttnam and chief ghostbuster Bill Murray. In a speech he made at a British–American chamber of commerce banquet Puttnam dismissed Murray as 'An actor who makes millions off movies but gives nothing back to his art. He's a taker.' Puttnam later insisted that he was misquoted, but nevertheless relations chilled between the two men. In 1987 Putnam was ousted and the first project on the desk of the new studio chief was the *Ghostbusters* sequel, so important was the picture for the financial survival of the company. Ironically, Murray himself was not exactly enamoured over the prospect of donning his proton-pack again, but he was persuaded to make the movie after a glitzy showbiz lunch organized by super agent Michael Ovitz.

Ghostbusters 2 isn't so much a sequel as a complete re-make of the first film. Whereas *Aliens* enlarged on its predecessor to the point of familiarity, presenting the audience with a completely new movie experience at the same time, Murray and the others took the easy route of just rehashing old ideas and situations, only less successfully. But the movie seems to work. *Ghostbusters 2* is fairly enjoyable stuff. It has no pretensions about being anything else but a huge, entertaining romp. But compared to the sparkling originality displayed in the earlier movie this is a tired and disappointing sequel. We are subjected to the same old stock jokes, a similar plot line and special effects. The Statue of Liberty climax, for example, is just a re-working of the more memorable Mr Stay-Puft sequence from the first film. As the story opens, the ghostbusters gang are back on the skids, five years after saving New York from eternal darkness. Venkman is the host of a crummy psychic cable talk-show, Stantz and Zeddmore demean themselves by re-enacting past glories at parties for ungrateful children, while Spengler has returned to his laboratory. As for Dana Barrett, she too has had her fair share of misfortune. A divorcée, Dana now has a small child by the name of Oscar. When her child is in danger of being sacrificed to give life to a long-dormant eighteenth-century Carpathian warlord the ghostbusters once again spring into action.

During the weeks of outdoor location work in the streets of New York, Sigourney was privy to some incredible sights of fan adulation. All around the cordoned-off Manhattan areas, hundreds of New Yorkers would gather, chanting the *Ghostbusters* theme. Groups of kids would point and shout with glee upon recognizing the actors. Back in the winter of 1983, during production of the first *Ghostbusters* film, Sigourney was a star in the making and something of a novice in the world of cinema, with only four movie appearances to her credit. But times had changed. Now she was a superstar of international prominence and an acclaimed actor. Although she received only third billing on *Ghostbusters 2*, she was undoubtedly the main star. Midway through the shooting, the Oscar nominations were announced and Sigourney found herself nominated in two acting categories, (for *Gorillas in the Mist* and *Working Girl*). This was an achievement that Bill Murray saw fit to ridicule for the rest of the filming. 'They tortured me, those guys,' recalled Sigourney in light jest. Whenever she seemed to be getting too serious in her acting for Murray's taste he would announce every time she walked onto the set, 'Here she comes, fellas, the two-time Oscar nominee herself.' Once, during a break from filming, Murray inexplicably began spitting hair balls at Sigourney, just like a cat. Ivan Reitman had to cut in and tell him to stop it. 'Bill thinks I'm too stiff and is continually freaking me out on the set,' Sigourney complained in a *Time Out* interview at the beginning of 1989. 'Hanging me upside down, tickling my nose.'

Ghostbusters 2 was released in America at a time when Columbia Pictures was in dire financial straits. A string of box-office disasters had lowered the company's credibility and they now badly needed a smash hit. A failure could spell the collapse of the studio. All hopes were pinned on *Ghostbusters 2* to deliver the goods. Luckily, the movie was an unqualified success and Columbia claimed the biggest ever three-day opening in cinema history, with box-office receipts in excess of $29 million. In the long term, however, the film fared less well than its illustrious predecessor. Critically, *Ghostbusters 2* was treated contemptuously. Many thought the movie too derivative, blatantly contrived and packaged for mass consumption. The *Financial Times*' opinion that the picture was 'long, witless and overproduced' was fairly indicative of the general antipathy towards this unwanted sequel.

After a batch of prestigious roles in highly acclaimed movies many of Sigourney's colleagues and critics felt the actress had lowered herself by appearing in such low-grade rubbish. During the inevitable publicity tour for the new film, Sigourney grew weary of defending her decision to rejoin the ghostbusters and make the commercially minded sequel. The money was certainly an inducement; she wasn't doing the movie for the artistic challenge; but she maintained that her involvement was precipitated by the audience's love for the characters and the joy of working with Murray and the boys again. (Prior to filming Sigourney sensed that the producers were far from keen on having her back in the cast, perhaps because she was now too expensive.) On a more personal level, as soon as she had heard that Dana Barrett was to be given a child she was immediately interested. For the past few years Sigourney and Jim Simpson had been trying desperately and without success to have a child. Yet the prospect of handling real live babies initially filled her with dread. She had never worked with them before. In the end, Sigourney figured that she had worked with baby gorillas and that perhaps the human variety were no different. In preparation for the maternal duties she would have to perform in front of the cameras, Sigourney practised bathing co-star Rick Moranis's new baby. The experience paid off, for when it came time to meet the seven-month-old twins William and Henry Deutschendorf, who were to play Oscar, Sigourney was surging with confidence. 'Holding a baby the right way up came much more naturally than I thought,' she disclosed to *You* magazine in December 1989. 'I guess instinct took over. In fact I found them very interesting little creatures.' Sigourney's on-screen role of mother turned out to be a dry run for the real thing. A few months after the June première of *Ghostbusters 2* Sigourney, to her obvious delight, was told that she was pregnant. By a strange coincidence, Dan Aykroyd's wife also had a baby, as did the wife of Harold Ramis. Perhaps working with the young Deutschendorf twins had an effect on them all. Sigourney was amused to learn from her doctor that she might even be expecting twins herself.

Sigourney Weaver has always been the kind of person for whom things happen too late in life. Irrespective of her fine and acknowledged work in the theatre Sigourney didn't become a household name until she was in her thirties – 'now motherhood in my forties, and to be honest I'm a little worried about the age gap between myself and my child'. However real her fears were at thirty-nine the actress had the financial and emotional security which allowed her to approach motherhood with a great deal of confidence. She decided to put her career on hold and take a year off to have her first child, a luxury few other women can afford. The prospect of motherhood radically changed Sigourney's outlook on life. She began to realize where her priorities lay and what was important. Work now came a poor second to the responsibilities of bringing up a child. She feels enormous sympathy and sadness for parents who postpone having children just to satisfy career demands. Prior to her long sabbatical a heavily pregnant Sigourney still managed a few publicity rounds, drumming up business for *Ghostbusters 2*. For journalists this was a rare chance to catch the mood and emotions of the mother-to-be. Generally she was taking things easy, spending her days reading a multitude of different books about birth and motherhood, filling her mind with theories about babies, and shopping around for maternity wear, a chore which she found both time-consuming and unpleasant. 'Maternity clothes are all so awful,' Sigourney complained to *You* magazine in November 1989. 'If I wear Laura Ashley stuff, being so tall, it makes me look like a kindergarten child in time warp.' Sigourney seemed to be having fun with her pregnancy.

After she had concluded her promotional duties for *Ghostbusters 2* Sigourney withdrew from the spotlight and disappeared from view. There were no films in the pipeline, no new challenging and ambitious roles on the horizon. Instead, Sigourney and Jim retired to their newly built home near the Canadian border ('I won't tell anybody where we are. Real estate is becoming synonymous with peace and quiet … '), where they planned to spend the majority of their time in lush solitude and tranquillity, at last beginning the family they had always dreamed of sharing.

Afterword

'I don't think it'll happen. I doubt there will be a third *Alien* movie. I don't know where you go next.'

An amazon woman brandishes a flame thrower deep within the bowels of an alien planetoid. She blasts out nitro-spurts of liquid fire into the menacing shadows and murky darkness before her. Ripley is back. It is ironic that Sigourney should choose to return to the cinema after a three year self-imposed exile in the role that originally made her a star, that of the liberated and gun-toting Ripley, in the wake of a new breed of action women. Hollywood has taken a long time to recognize the fact that the techno-schlock militarist woman is an appealing and bankable commodity. In recent years there has been a veritable flood of no-nonsense female warriors who shoot first and ask questions later. A response one might think to the rise of the New Age wimp typified by Kevin Costner and Alec Baldwin, and the perennial Hollywood stereotyping of women in film. Linda Hamilton's survivalist mother in *Terminator 2* (ironically directed by James Cameron, who was so influential in the development of the Ripley character) is a prime example of this nineties trend, but there are others from Mary Elizabeth Mastrantonio's tough Maid Marian to *Thelma and Louise*.

These new *femmes fatales* owe much to the tough image that Sigourney made her own as Ripley. They too dish out heavy-duty violence while retaining their femininity and sex appeal. They are also ripped straight from the tabloid and hard-news images of Middle Eastern female commandos and the nefarious women terrorists of the seventies: Ulrike Meinhof and Patty Hearst. For decades women have been poorly served by a male dominated film industry. Very few actresses get the chance to play much more than the hero's girlfriend or a persecuted (usually at the hands of a man) victim. Times have changed, but turning them into Rambos surely isn't the answer, merely a short-term solution. It does reflect, however, a growing desire on the part of women to take more control, and Sigourney for one has always welcomed such opportunities.

When principal photography commenced on *Alien 3* at Pinewood studios on 14 January 1991 Sigourney hadn't made a film for two years. Her talent had been sorely missed from the screen. (In Sigourney's absence she and others of her generation, Streep *et al.*, have been usurped by a new breed of actress, notably Julia Roberts and Annette Benning, who now battle it out for supremacy as top female box office draw). Following the success of *Ghostbusters 2* Sigourney Weaver vanished from the cinema, leaving her fans feeling cheated and betrayed. This long sabbatical was taken just when her career seemed at last on course for greatness and she had attained international stardom and overwhelming critical praise for her performances in *Gorillas in the Mist* and *Working Girl*. Sigourney's admirers have always thought that the actress doesn't do enough regular film work and they would like to see her make at least one movie a year. In the winter of 1989 Sigourney was scheduled to play a major role in *The Handmaid's Tale*, a disturbing film based on Margaret Atwood's sci-fi shocker which tells of a future society that has regressed into the past, particularly in its attitude towards women and their place in society. Sigourney was keen on taking part and talked with enthusiasm about the project to journalists. 'Very interesting, very scary. If it comes off it won't be exactly funny, but it will I hope be compelling.' In the end Sigourney's pregnancy ruled out all possibilities of appearing in the film, which upon release was slated anyway. Now all scripts and offers of work were temporarily put to one side. Sigourney's professional life, to all intents and purposes, was in limbo. It was her personal life that now took centre stage.

In preparation of the birth of their child Sigourney and Jim Simpson acquired a luxurious new home on the outskirts of New York and waited. A few months into the new decade, April to be exact, Sigourney gave birth to a little girl, christened Charlotte, in a New York hospital. Her life was now complete. Sigourney had been a film star for ten years and now at the age of forty she was at last a mother. It would be a touch cliché to say that baby Charlotte changed Sigourney Weaver's life overnight, but the child was certainly responsible for instilling within her mother a restored sense of optimism. 'Having a baby makes me think more of the future.' The daughter of showbiz parents herself, Sigourney often wonders how her own stardom will affect Charlotte. 'I hope she won't be too interested in what Mommy does for a living for a while.' She cannot, for instance, certainly in the near future, envisage a time when she would allow Charlotte to view the *Alien* trilogy. Sigourney has met little kids in America who are avid fans of the films, but there are those who find them disturbing to watch. One is reminded about the tale of Margaret Hamilton, the actress who played the green-faced, hook-nosed wicked witch in *The Wizard of Oz*, who never allowed her children to watch the picture; she was very protective about it. Her daughter eventually saw the film at a friend's house and was horrified and shocked to see her mother performing a host of atrocities. Sigourney doesn't want such a thing happening to her, and so is probably prepared to let Charlotte watch *Alien* when she reaches the ripe old age of ten or eleven. But not until then.

Relatively isolated in their new home from the furious world of movie-making, Sigourney and Jim lavished all their love and energy on raising their first child. 'I'm loving it here with us all together, but I'm getting ready to go back to work now.' For some time Sigourney had let it be known that she was potentially available for *Alien 3* if the package of script, director and fee met with her approval. The actress quite rightly views the success and popularity of the *Alien* series as enhancing her bankability for more offbeat projects. *Alien 3* had been lumbering towards production since early 1989, under the weight of numerous scripts (about five in total, some of which didn't even feature the character of Ripley) and directors. One storyline had the monster running amok inside a floating prison ship.

In January 1991 Sigourney arrived at Heathrow airport to begin work on the biggest and most fantastical movie of her career, so far. Along for the ride was baby Charlotte. Instead of the traditional pram Sigourney was often sighted carrying her daughter in a sling, 'my little papoose' and uncharacteristically was willing to be photographed on arrival with her pride and joy. There was something else visibly different about Sigourney as she waltzed through the world's busiest terminal. Her hair, it had gone. Those dark flowing locks had been left behind in America and she was now sporting a crew cut, a severe look which didn't suit her at all. Indeed it made her face appear gaunt and skeletal-like. But this new image was an essential part of the film and Sigourney's co-stars, Charles Dance and Paul McGann, had also made drastic visits to the barber.

Following *Aliens* in 1986 Sigourney told reporters that she would never again be playing Ripley. 'The prospect of doing another *Alien* doesn't exactly bowl me over. Ripley is almost too familiar.' Five years later on a sound stage at Pinewood she was back. Why? 'It's a wonderful story and that's the most important thing, otherwise none of us would have gone near it.' Behind closed doors and under a cloak of secrecy cameras rolled on *Alien 3*. The film's intricate storyline was so hush-hush that even some members of the cast were not privy to the full script. After Ridley Scott and James Cameron, previous directors for the series, 20th Century Fox seemed to be taking an almighty risk in allowing a relatively inexperienced new director, David Fincher, take the helm of what was an expensive and important enterprise. Fincher was responsible for Madonna's celebrated monochrome *Vogue* video. *Alien 3* marks his feature film début. Sigourney, however, has every confidence in the young man and is clearly excited about what will certainly prove to be the final instalment in the *Alien* saga. 'It'll be good, real scary. This film will be the last though, I'm not Sylvester Stallone.' Fans around the world will surely mourn the loss of Ripley, a character that like it or not Sigourney will be forever identified with.

Throughout her career Sigourney's achievements in the field of acting, her two Oscar nominations and a string of hit movies, have been underlined by the nagging suspicion that what she is doing for a living isn't really important. An actor is merely 'a hired hand' as she rather bluntly puts it. The desire to find more constructive and significant outlets for her talents has been with Sigourney almost from the beginning of her career. One recurring ambition is to produce a film of her father holding a series of lectures about the future of television. Perhaps now she has her own production company, that ultimate confirmation of success, this and other similarly worthy projects will see the light of day.

Goat Cay productions was conceived in January 1988 when Sigourney's agent, Sam Cohn, introduced the actress to the influential Jerry Weintraub. For Sigourney the lure of producing is simple to understand. It's all about power. As an independent producer she is, in effect, the decision maker, the one who calls the shots. 'I want to be the producer so that I am listened to on things that affect the way the audience perceives my work.' Sigourney cherishes an admittedly idealistic notion that the true job of a producer is to see that the artistic integrity of a film is not compromised in any way. A case in point was *Half Moon Street*. The director, Bob Swaim, lost creative control of the picture and was continually in fierce conflict with the money men. A good and seasoned producer would have made sure that all financial matters were his responsibility, thus leaving the director free to concentrate on making art (or trash in the case of *Half Moon Street*). As 'a hired hand' Sigourney has encountered problems on every one of her twelve films. If she could go back, in the guise of producer, there are many things the actress would change. She would have made sure the actors on *Alien* were treated more respectfully, allowed William Hurt and herself to experiment with more on-camera improvisation during the shooting of *The Janitor*, given herself a better bite of the comedy pie in *Deal of the Century* and made *Half Moon Street* a much tougher and uncompromising film and endowed her character with a more pronounced sense of humour. In *Aliens* she would have kept in the reference to Ripley's lost daughter and removed the music of Maurice Jarre from *Gorillas in the Mist*. In her opinion Jarre's soundtrack was 'intrusive and overdone'. Most importantly of all Sigourney would have battled long and hard to keep *Lone Star* afloat.

With the help of Weintraub, Sigourney was able to set herself up as a producer in her own company. The marriage between artist and businessman, however, was an uneasy one. Sigourney wanted to pursue highbrow projects: a film based on a Mishima play and an anarchic comedy, while Weintraub was looking for family orientated commercial properties. 'I could tell from the contract,' Sigourney told *Première* magazine in October 1988, 'that they were not interested in some muse coming in and doing something high and mighty.' Today Goat Cay is still very much a going concern, despite the fact that nothing material has emerged from them as yet. Perhaps the nineties will see Sigourney concentrating more on the production side of cinema. (Immediately after the completion of *Alien 3* she returned to New York to start work on various project ideas.) Sigourney is destined, it seems, to spend the future just as much behind the camera as in front of it. As she herself confesses 'I'm not very good about being a movie star'. Sigourney has always been curiously modest about her own acting accomplishments. 'I don't feel I have any real gift for it. I think I am definitely a person who has learned how to do it.'

As Sigourney Weaver continues to mature and flourish as a leading/character actress in the same vein as Katharine Hepburn and Jane Fonda, one gets the distinct impression that we haven't seen the best of her yet. Sigourney, however, has her own private ambition. 'Well, I've always admired Margaret Rutherford. Like her I'd like to play Miss Marple when I'm eighty.' Now wouldn't that be a sight worth waiting for.

Filmography

Annie Hall (1977)

Director: Woody Allen
Producer: Charles H. Joffe
Screenplay: Woody Allen and Marshall Brickman
Photography: Gordon Willis
Studio: United Artists
Running Time: 93 minutes
Certificate: AA

Cast: Woody Allen, Dian Keaton, Tony Roberts, Paul Simon, Carol Kane, Shelley Duvall, Janet Margolin, Christopher Walken, Colleen Dewhurst, Jeff Goldblum, Sigourney Weaver

Release Date: USA: March 1977/UK: October 1977

Alien (1979)

Director: Ridley Scott
Producer: Gordon Carroll
Screenplay: Dan O'Bannon
Photography: Derek Vanlint
Music: Jerry Goldsmith
Studio: 20th Century-Fox
Running Time: 117 minutes
Certificate: X

Cast: Tom Skerritt, Sigourney Weaver, Veronica Cartwright, Harry Dean Stanton, John Hurt, Ian Holm, Yaphet Kotto

Release Date: USA: May 1979/UK: September 1979

The Janitor (1981); USA title: **Eyewitness**

Director: Peter Yates
Producer: Peter Yates
Screenplay: Steve Tesich
Photography: Matthew F. Leonetti
Music: Stanley Silverman
Studio: 20th Century-Fox
Running Time: 102 minutes
Certificate: AA

Cast: William Hurt, Sigourney Weaver, Christopher Plummer, James Woods, Irene Worth, Kenneth McMillan, Pamela Reed, Morgan Freeman

Release Date: USA: March 1981/UK: October 1981

The Year of Living Dangerously (1983)

Director: Peter Weir
Producer: James McElroy
Screenplay: David Williamson, Peter Weir, C.J. Koch
Photography: Russell Boyd
Music: Maurice Jarre
Studio: MGM/UA
Running Time: 115 minutes
Certificate: PG

Cast: Mel Gibson, Sigourney Weaver, Linda Hunt, Bembol Roco, Michael Murphy, Noel Ferrier, Bill Kerr

Release Date: USA: January 1983/UK: June 1983

Deal of the Century (1983)

Director: William Friedkin
Producer: Bud Yorkin
Screenplay: Paul Brickman
Photography: Richard H. Kline
Music: Arthur B. Rubinstein
Studio: Warner Brothers
Running Time: 98 minutes
Certificate: 15

Cast: Chevy Chase, Sigourney Weaver, Gregory Hines, Vince Edwards, Wallace Shawn

Release Date: USA: November 1983/not theatrically released in British theatres

Ghostbusters (1984)

Director: Ivan Reitman
Producer: Ivan Reitman
Screenplay: Dan Aykroyd and Harold Ramis
Photography: Laszlo Kovacs
Music: Elmer Bernstein
Studio: Columbia
Running Time: 107 minutes
Certificate: PG

Cast: Bill Murray, Dan Aykroyd, Harold Ramis, Sigourney Weaver, Rick Moranis, Annie Potts, Ernie Hudson, William Atherton

Release Date: USA: June 1984/UK: December 1984

A Woman or Two (1985); USA Title: *One Woman or Two*

Director: Daniel Vigne
Producer: Philippe Dussart
Screenplay: Daniel Vigne and Elisabeth Rappeneau
Photography: Carlo Varini
Music: Kevin Mulligan
Running Time: 97 minutes
Certificate: 15

Cast: Gerard Depardieu, Sigourney Weaver, Ruth Westheimer, Michel Aumont

Release Date: USA: February 1987/UK: June 1986

Half Moon Street (1986)

Director: Bob Swaim
Producer: Geoffrey Reeve

Screenplay: Bob Swaim and Edward Behr
Photography: Peter Hannan
Music: Richard Harvey
Studio: RKO
Running Time: 89 minutes
Certificate: 18

Cast: Sigourney Weaver, Michael Caine, Patrick Kavanagh, Keith Buckley, Patrick Newman, Nadim Sawalha, Maria Aitken

Release Date: USA: September 1986/UK: April 1987

Aliens (1986)

Director: James Cameron
Producer: Gale Anne Hurd
Screenplay: James Cameron
Photography: Adrian Biddle
Music: James Horner
Studio: 20th Century-Fox
Running Time: 137 minutes
Certificate: 18

Cast: Sigourney Weaver, Carrie Henn, Michael Biehn, Paul Reiser, Lance Henriksen, Bill Paxton

Release Date: USA: July 1986/UK: August 1986

Gorillas in the Mist (1988)

Director: Michael Apted
Producer: Arnold Glimcher
Screenplay: Anna Hamilton Phelan
Photography: John Seale
Music: Maurice Jarre
Studio: Warner Bros./Universal
Running Time: 129 minutes
Certificate: 15

Cast: Sigourney Weaver, Bryan Brown, Julie Harris, John Omirah Miluwi, Iain Cuthbertson

Release Date: USA: September 1988/UK: January 1989

Working Girl (1988)

Director: Mike Nichols
Producer: Douglas Wick
Screenplay: Kevin Wade
Photography: Michael Ballhaus
Music: Carly Simon
Studio: 20th Century Fox
Running Time: 113 Minutes
Certificate: 15

Cast: Harrison Ford, Sigourney Weaver, Melanie Griffith, Alec Baldwin, Joan Cusack, Philip Bosco, Olympia Dukakis

Release Date: USA: December 1988/ UK: April 1989

Ghostbusters II (1989)

Director: Ivan Reitman
Producer: Ivan Reitman
Screenplay: Harold Ramis and Dan Aykroyd
Photography: Michael Chapman
Music: Randy Edelman
Studio: Columbia
Running Time: 102 minutes
Certificate: PG

Cast: Bill Murray, Dan Aykroyd, Sigourney Weaver, Harold Ramis, Rick Moranis, Ernie Hudson, Peter MacNicol, Annie Potts

Release Date: USA: June 1989/UK: December 1989

Alien III (1992)

Director: David Fincher

Cast: Sigourney Weaver, Charles Dance, Charles Dutton, Paul McGann, Brian Glover

Index